Please
Don't Let Me Be the Oldest Mom in the PTA

stories about mid-life motherhood

Please
Don't Let Me Be the Oldest Mom in the PTA

stories about mid-life motherhood

Sharon O'Donnell

Torchflame Books
An imprint of Light Messages
Durham, NC

Published 2018, by Torchflame Books
    an Imprint of Light Messages
www.lightmessages.com
Durham, NC 27713 USA
SAN: 920-9298

Paperback ISBN: 978-1-61153-289-0
E-book ISBN: 978-1-61153-288-3
Library of Congress Control Number: 2018937952

Dedicated to my mother, Wiloree,
who had me when she was 38;
my father, Sam, who was the 11th of 12 children;
and to my three sons, Billy, David,
and last but most certainly not least,
Jason, my caboose baby.

Contents

Acknowledgements

This book was an idea that started after having my third son, Jason, who was nine years younger than my oldest son and six years younger than my middle son. Definitely a 'caboose' baby. And there were noticeable differences in motherhood the third time around. It's been ten years since my first humor book, House of Testosterone, was released by Houghton Mifflin; during that time, my husband, sons, and I have lived life with all of its joys and challenges. I'm back now to share these experiences and to hope they resonate in some way with you.

I'd like to thank my husband, Kevin, and my sons, Billy, David, and Jason for not thinking I'm totally nuts staying up writing until three in the morning. I appreciate their support and the plethora of anecdotes that they have unwittingly provided to me as writing material. I'd also like to thank my parents, Sam & Wiloree Johnson, and my three siblings for the family life I had growing up and for their encouraging and believing in me. Our parents are truly remarkable and have been such wonderful role models for each of us. Thank you to Claire for adding some estrogen to our house of testosterone the past eight years, and I'm so glad you and David met way back in 10th grade. To my friends Michelle, Robyn, Amy, and Tina for always being there to talk to or to have a much-needed girls' night out. Thanks to Elizabeth Harrison,

Amy Wiley, and Karen Noreen for reading my manuscript and providing feedback.

For the past eight years, I've often blogged for motherhoodlater.com, which is a comprehensive website for older moms; Robin Gorman Newman is the founder of this wonderful site, and I'd like to thank her for her support and encouragement over the years. I really appreciate Light Messages for giving me the opportunity to reach other 'older' moms through my book. As always, I thank God for giving me the innate desire to write because it is my passion.

Introduction

Older moms are a rapidly growing segment of the population. They call us "Advanced Maternal Age." Yes, we have been dubbed. I hate it when I'm dubbed, don't you?

—Sharon O'Donnell

Motherhood is not what it used to be. Statistics show that more moms are having children later in life than ever before, a fact that's obvious by simply taking a look around at playgrounds, day care centers, and PTA meetings. Older moms are everywhere! This book is for all those moms with that deer in the headlights look who suddenly discover that breastfeeding and AARP membership aren't that far apart. For me, it was indeed a startling revelation that I had to navigate my son through kindergarten while at the same time deal with my body going through changes and challenges I'd never envisioned.

But what should people call that group of older moms? An article in *The Arizona Republic* back in 2005 highlighted the fact that the number of older moms was steadily increasing and that the medical community had "dubbed" these women "advanced maternal age." So there you have it: we have been dubbed. I hate being dubbed, don't you? Especially when it's with a title like "advanced maternal age." The first time in my life I've been advanced at something, thank you very much. The term 'mid-life mom' is becoming rather popular, and it certainly sounds better than Advanced Maternal Age. What about Above Average Age moms? Or hey, how about just something simple like "older moms." "Advanced maternal age" makes it sound like a chronic illness, not simply women over 35 who have babies. Some websites call us later in life moms or seasoned moms, both of which have a much nicer ring to it than advanced maternal age. Anything with the word 'maternal' in it is not going to be self-esteem building or flattering—conjures up images of women in plain, brown Little House on the Prairie dresses. Sexy! I've even heard us called—get this—geriatric moms. That one sounds like we are putting in dentures while nursing our babies. Word choice, people, it's all about word choice. Some folks in the medical community could definitely use a thesaurus.

Let us dub ourselves please. There are plenty of choices here, medical community take notice! Is there such a moniker for *men* who father babies when they are older, sometimes much, much older than the average dad? Oh yes, that's right—stud. What a double standard that is! Exactly who is this "medical community" that gets to label us?

But it's clear that the medical community is grasping for a label for us older moms because there's a dire need for a title of our growing segment of the population. Our numbers are increasing rapidly. 2014 numbers from the National Vital Statistics Report show that more women over age 40 are having children, as compared with lower numbers for women in their twenties and teens. According to a 2010 study based on data from the National Center for Health Statistics and the U.S. Census Bureau, motherhood in America changed a lot from 1990 to 2008. One of the differences that stood out was:

Birth rates for women aged 35 to 39 increased by 47 percent, and rates for women aged 40 to 44 increased by 80 percent over the time period.[1]

Yes, moms are indeed getting older, and even though it's a struggle at times, I'm proud to be one of them. Many of these moms have older children and then have another child years later, like I did. When I had my last son at age 38, my husband and I had two other children already, ages nine and six. I loved the newest addition to our family, but there was also a sense of 'been there, done that.' After all, how many years of Cub Scout meetings or t-ball games can one person endure without going totally off the deep end?

Some of these older moms are first-time moms, taking on the novice territory of parenthood later than most. Yet, there is a common bond that all older moms share: they are facing the challenges of raising children while they themselves are in the midst of physical and emotional changes that growing older brings. It's about taking care of a child while tending to the needs of an older self.

Older moms face all of this, while battling the expectations and preconceived notions of what the mother of a young child should look like. The older mom club is not exactly a flattering, self-esteem-enhancing club to be a member of, thanks to society's obsession with youth. Though most of us are thrilled to become moms

---

1   Pew Research Center study. https://www.livescience.com/9903-today-amerhttps://www.livescience.com/9903-to-day-american-moms-older-educated.html

regardless of our age, older moms do face some prejudices and challenges—while also reaping tremendous rewards. Nothing like holding a baby in your arms at any age.

With this book, I hope to connect with moms who have had a child after age 35, the age at which obstetricians and gynecologists think our bodies will fall apart and our eggs dry up and thus, label these as high risk pregnancies.

Allow me to share an excerpt from my book *House of Testosterone* about the moment I knew I wanted to have a third child:

When I was 36, I went in for my annual gynecological exam and had to see the new doctor, a man in his late twenties, who also happened to be very attractive, which can be rather embarrassing in that situation. I sat in a chair as he looked over my chart. Then he turned to me and said, "Soooo...I guess your childbearing years are over." He posed it partly as a question and partly as an indisputable fact. I had a powerful urge to reply, "Yep, that's right. Just put me out to pasture with Old Nellie. We're off to the glue factory now." I swore I could feel my ovaries drying up as I sat in his office chair, my eggs being zapped by a microscopic laser gun with a neon light flashing "Game Over!"

This new book is for women who have had moments like that. It's for all those moms out there who have mistakenly been called their kid's grandma. For the moms who had children when they were younger, only to have another child after turning 40. For all those moms who have been in the trenches and then just when they were about to climb out ... they went back in again. For all those moms who have one child entering college, one child in high school, and ... a second grader. And this book is for all those moms who experience motherhood for the first time when they are over the ripe old age of 35. For all those moms who would like to pay for a facelift or some Botox but instead have to pay for their youngest kid's braces or back surgery for themselves. For all the moms who know our wrinkles come from the things our kids put us through, the frown lines and the laugh lines. And this book is for all the moms who are growing older in a houseful of guys who cannot empathize at all with irregular periods or how harrowing it is the first time you see those little lines by your mouth. For all those moms who desperately pray on the way to the first PTA meeting of the year, "Please, God, don't let me be the oldest mom there."

So older moms, here is a book just for you about moments both embarrassing and poignant that all older moms can relate to. Perhaps someday it will be available in a large print vision. Until then, just squint. Or buy one of those magnifiers with the light on it—I have extra if you need one.

Sure Signs You are a Mom of a Certain Age

- You notice that all TV programs you watch have commercials for incontinence or the Scooter Store.
- You dread going to bed because of all the stuff you have to put on your face at night. And on your neck. And on your décolleté. Who the heck knew they even had a décolleté? I didn't until I heard it on one of those infomercials for wrinkle cream. Basically, it's your neck and cleavage area.

Yet another body area we are expected to keep smooth and firm. Damn it.

- You swallow your pride and go ahead and buy the damn bathing suit with the skirt.

- You wonder who in the hell set up the early starting times for middle school and high school because you are running on fumes. They talk about TEENS needing their sleep?

- You call the tanning salon and ask if you can tan your legs without tanning your face because you don't want to get any more wrinkles.

- You wear large necklaces just to distract people from looking at your face too closely.

- You find yourself taking your 10 year old son and your 85 year-old mother on vacation together. Sandwich generation vacation.

- When you get up from the bleachers at your child's basketball game, your knees won't cooperate like they used to.

- Your period is now more like a comma—or a question mark.

- You always take your sunglasses with you to hide your droopy eyelids in case someone takes a photo.

- Your bathroom cabinet contains sensitive toothpaste, Ibuprofen, Tylenol, Aleve, Excedrin Migraine, Excedrin Tension Headache, Excedrin Back & Body Aches, fish oil, and 20 different kinds of wrinkle cream.

- The teen idol you used to have a crush on when you were little is now 75 years old.

- You sometimes forget to make dinner for your youngest child since he's the only one left at home.
- You watch those Extreme Makeover shows and write down contact information for the plastic surgeons.
- You know just enough about social media to accidentally 'like' something on Twitter or Instagram that embarrasses your teenager.
- Your purse is the size of carry-on airplane luggage.
- You get really pissed off when the female store clerk—who looks about your age—calls you "sweetie".
- Your make-up concealer you used to dab on your face here and there to cover the flaws has suddenly become your overall foundation.
- You switch from an OB/GYN to just a GYN.
- You cannot be trusted with a credit card during Infomercials about wrinkles or weight loss.
- You haven't read directions for anything the past three years because the print is too damn small.

1
A Mom of a 'Certain Age'

I had my kids late. I didn't think I could have them and I didn't expect to have them. But they are my best work.

—Susan Sarandon

The PTA Meeting

When my youngest son, Jason, was born in 2000, I was 38 years old and thus, officially became an older mom since the field of medicine has decided that any mom giving birth or adopting after the age of 35 is considered older. Gee, thanks, medical field. My husband, Kevin, and I had two other sons already, ages nine and six. So I've been a younger mom as well as an older mom, and there is definitely a difference in how people perceived me the third time around. I've had kids in high school, middle school, and elementary school all at the same time. Homework on the same night included both calculus and multiplication tables with some algebra thrown in for the middle son. It was a wide range to cover, and it was challenging going back through the same things years after going through it the first two times.

PTA meetings the third time around with Jason, was not high on my 'to do' list when he got to elementary school. The main reason, as I told the principal, was that I was burned out from being so active with my other two sons' PTAs over the years, and I felt I just needed a break during Jason's kindergarten year. I'd organized fundraisers, edited newsletters, been the room mom, spearheaded Drug Awareness Red Ribbon week and arts contests, and many other projects. Of course, I'd support all of these events again, but taking a leadership position in the PTA was not something I felt I could do again at that time.

The PTA is a wonderful organization that enhances the educational experience of students and teachers, while also engaging the family and community. I was proud to have been so involved over the years in such a worthy mission, but I'd had children in school a decade already, and I was running low on energy.

The other reason I was hesitant to attend a PTA meeting was because I felt out of place at events where it was quite possible I'd be the oldest mom there. There is a nine-year-age gap between my oldest and youngest son, so being the oldest mom at Jason's elementary school events was a very real possibility. It's human nature to be self-conscious about things that others probably don't even notice. To me, I felt like as soon as I walked in the room, the other moms would immediately notice my age and wonder why I had a child who was so young. Just something I'd rather avoid if I could.

When Jason was in the first grade, I finally had the guts to attend a PTA meeting at his school. Well, actually, it wasn't so much my guts as the fact that Jason's class was also singing at this particular meeting, which meant I was expected to go. Having various classes perform at PTA meetings is a brilliant idea that someone hatched to make sure people attended the meetings because they'd want to go see little Johnny or Jenny sing. And that ploy is what got me there on that fateful night.

A few days before I went, I got my regular hair coloring done so no gray strands would show. The night of the meeting, I carefully reapplied my make-up, putting lots of concealer under my eyes and lengthening mascara on my stubby lashes. Then I put on a pair of jeans that didn't look like 'mom' jeans and a sweater that didn't scream, "I love the '80s."

So there I was finally walking into a PTA meeting filled with parents who probably couldn't even vaguely remember the Nixon administration and first watched The Brady Bunch in syndication, rather than the original run of the show on Friday nights on ABC. I was from another generation there amidst the cute, bubbly women in form-fitting jeans and capris with tans and no age spots. Moms with no spider veins. Moms who didn't need to hold the meeting agenda at arm's length to be able to read it. Moms with genuine enthusiasm for the upcoming magazine fundraiser. Before the meeting started, I hung around near the back of the room, trying not to draw attention to myself.

I enjoyed the performance, although I realized, as all the younger moms aimed their state-of-the-art mini VCRs at their little American Idols, that I had forgotten my own clunky video camera at home. That's another thing about being an older mom with age-gap kids: with my older boys, I was so prepared for things like school concerts—battery charged, extra tape, the whole works. Yet, with the third child, I'd had other things on my mind like helping my middle son study for a science test or picking up my oldest son from basketball practice; remembering a video camera on the way out the door is sometimes simply too much to ask. In the future, I will have to explain to Jason why there is a lot more video of his brothers' school programs than his.

After the school concert at the PTA meeting, there were some brief business topics discussed and something about new playground equipment was voted on. Afterwards, everyone was invited to have cookies and punch and to mingle. I didn't want to be anti-social, but I really didn't feel much like mingling that night, particularly with other moms who might not even have been born the year I graduated from high school.

And then I saw her across the crowded room, sitting near the stage. (Cue violin music). A kindred spirit. She was an attractive brunette, but it was obvious from some wrinkles and bit of turkey neck sag that she was at least as old as I was. Maybe—dare I say it—older?? My heart started beating fast like it used to when I'd see a cute guy taller than me out at the nightclubs. I had to meet her.

Then a boy named Mark from Jason's class went running over to the woman and hugged her. Ah, even better. Another older mom in the very same class. Play dates with him would be so much easier than those set up with moms ten years younger. While the boys played, we could discuss IRA accounts, hot flashes, and how Tom Selleck still looked so good, all while laughing at the unjaded enthusiasm of the younger moms. We'd have a wonderful time together.

When Jason came off the stage, I made it a point that he and I walked past Mark and the woman. "So you're Mark's mom," I said, smiling. "Jason is in his class."

She smiled back. "Actually, I'm his grandmother," she replied. "My daughter couldn't be here tonight so I'm filling in."

Holy crap. I felt my face fall even lower than normal. She wasn't a kindred spirit at all; she was a young grandmother! My kindred spirit fantasy suddenly went poof! in a cloud of fairy dust. I tried not to act surprised or disappointed by her revelation. "Oh," I said nonchalantly, and then made some comment about Jason really liking the songs they sang that night. I made polite chit-chat as we made our way out of the room. Then I grabbed Jason by the arm and fled out a side door.

So you see why I'm inclined to shy away from meetings with the parents of Jason's peers. How do I explain this PTA phobia of mine to others? Unless they were born before 1970, I don't bother. The key for me is to volunteer to help in the classroom but not to commit to attending meetings with lots of other people in well-lit rooms where there'd be the possibility of being under scrutiny. But perhaps one day, I'll find a mom who is my kindred spirit—my fellow 'born in the sixties brethren"—trying to be inconspicuous as I am, hiding in the back of the meeting room.

My oldest sister Gail also had her third son when she was in her late thirties, and I remember her telling me—a naïve newlywed then—how old she felt doing things with him compared to doing things with her first two sons. I thought she was overreacting and downplayed her feelings with a dismissive wave of my hand. But I understand now exactly how my sister felt as I drive reluctantly to Jason's school for a meeting, thinking the whole time, "Please God, don't let me be the oldest mom in the PTA!"

The Burned-Out Tooth Fairy

Is there a mandatory retirement age for Tooth Fairies? I think there should be. I played Tooth Fairy for many years, first with Billy, my oldest son, then with David, my middle one, and then with Jason. How many baby teeth do kids have anyway? With Jason, I was too old to remember to replace the tooth with money under his pillow before I went to bed and definitely too old to get up in the middle of the night to do it because I forgot earlier. And with the older two boys to deal with at the same time, I had more important things on my mind like SATs, GPAs, and girlfriends, so remembering Jason's lost tooth would sometimes slip my mind. I've written about my Tooth Fairy experiences before, but there always seems to be another tooth adventure around the corner for me. One such adventure involved Jason's silver tooth.

First though, a little background on Jason's dental history. When he was little, he'd do great when he went in for a cleaning, but cavities, sealants, or x-rays were pure torture for him—and me—and everyone in the dental office. A definite candidate for sedation dentistry. He had allergies and a gag reflex that made dental procedures difficult. Jason had trouble breathing during these procedures, resulting in him getting very upset and breaking into tears and screams. He was the one I absolutely dreaded taking to the dentist. When the dental staff would see Jason come in for something other than a cleaning, they would immediately call—or ahem—draft, a second hygienist to help out. Yep, the whole dental staff knew my boy well.

So when I found out 6-year-old Jason would have to have a silver tooth, akin to an adult's crown, I wasn't thrilled. I felt guilty, too, because I hadn't been as diligent about brushing Jason's teeth as I had been with my older boys; but, with Jason, I was always so concerned about his allergies and eczema, that his teeth had taken a back seat. There would be the dentist in the small, separate room along with two dental hygienists who would help me hold him down (Jason, not the dentist). Not a relaxing way to spend an afternoon. The hygienists and dentist were always great with Jason, but there was only so much they could do for him when he panicked the way he did. Between sobs and screams, he yelled, "I can't breathe!"

I leaned over, still holding his hand, and patted his other arm. "It'll be okay, sweetie," I tried to calm him. I hated seeing him so upset, but nothing I said or did could soothe him. My heart was breaking for him, and tears formed in my own eyes. This scene went on for a few more minutes as I watched them work inside Jason's mouth. I could see they were putting a silver contraption of some sort in his mouth, so I was hopeful this was what they used to press the crown in place and that the procedure would be over soon. Then they started polishing the silver, and it dawned on me that this huge hunk of silver was actually Jason's new tooth. This caught me off guard because I'd been expecting an enamel-colored crown like most adults get. Just to make sure, I asked hesitantly, "Are you going to leave that in there?"

"Ah, well, that's his tooth," the dentist said gently. He realized I'd been expecting something different and explained that kids usually have silver crowns because the tooth will come out within a few years and are less expensive. I knew that made sense, but that didn't change the fact that Jason had a hunk of silver on the side of his mouth, visible when he smiled big.

Later as we exited the office, I wanted to make sure Jason understood that he now had a silver tooth; I didn't want him to freak out when he saw it in the mirror for the first time. "Jason," I began, bracing myself for his tears, "you do know you have a silver tooth now?"

He looked at me, startled. Then he said, "Cool! Emily's got a silver tooth." I sighed in relief and thanked God for his school friend Emily. As he climbed into the car, Jason reached for the mirror on the visor and grinned, admiring the shiny metal. It all turned out okay, but the next time, Jason had to go to the dentist, it was for X-rays, a definite gag inciter, so I scheduled it on a day I was teaching a writing class and my husband, Kevin, would have to take him. Honestly, I couldn't wait for Kevin to see what I'd had to put up with at Jason's dentist appointments for the past several years; he'd then definitely appreciate the contributions of this stay-at-home mom. At the end of the day, I couldn't wait to ask Kevin how it went. To my surprise, he shrugged and said, "Jason was great."

"What?!" I asked, totally stunned.

"He behaved very well," Kevin replied. "Nothing to it," he added with a nonchalant flip of his hand, as he turned back to the computer. I steadied myself against the wall, flabbergasted. I looked over at the couch where Jason sat watching TV. He grinned at me, as if he knew he'd just bested me in a battle.

"What did you say to him?" I asked Kevin.

"I just said, 'Get your butt up there, Twerp, and behave.'"

I stared at Jason, my feelings hurt. All this time, I'd tried to be nurturing to him and supportive by saying things like "I'll be right beside you" and "It'll all be over soon".

And then his dad tells him to get his butt up there and those are the blankin' magic words?

About a year and a half later when Jason was almost eight, the silver tooth came out since it was a baby tooth. Of course, it came out near bedtime and Kevin was out of town, which meant I, the Tooth Fairy, wasn't prepared. I knew I had no $1 or $5 bills in the house, and I wasn't about to give him anything larger. That had happened previously and giving $10 because that's all you have in the house sets a bad precedent for future lost teeth gifts. So after Jason was asleep, I ran through the house lifting up seat cushions and looking under tables, trying to find enough quarters to make five dollars.

At that point, I contemplated just going ahead and telling Jason the truth about the Tooth Fairy; surely, I thought, he'd heard rumors. Perhaps it was just time for the talk, and it would make my life a lot easier. I suspect part of the reason I felt that way was after three sons, I was simply burned out on the Tooth Fairy routine. Tooth Fairies should be much younger than I am to really be at the top of their game. Yet, I hated to tell Jason the truth. In this day and age, I felt that the Tooth Fairy was a part of a fleeting innocence, and I wasn't ready for Jason to leave that stage of his life yet.

So I kept foraging for coins. After an exhaustive search, discovering a pacifier from six years earlier, and raiding my older two sons' wallets, I'd found the 20 quarters I needed. I felt an adrenalin rush like a big game hunter might feel once the hunt was successful. Looking at all those shiny coins, I could just imagine them rolling out from under his pillow, so I put them all in a plastic baggie. Jason was sleeping with me that particular night since Kevin was out of town, and Jason asks to sleep in our bed sometimes on what he declares as 'special' nights. Losing a tooth qualified as such a night. I slid the bag under the pillow and drifted off to sleep.

In the middle of the night, there was a thud, and I realized the money bag had fallen through the crack between the mattress and the headboard. I could either get up then and fish it out or I could wait until the morning. Like any sane person, I decided to wait. When Jason awoke, his hand immediately went under the pillow, and he exclaimed, "Hey the Tooth Fairy didn't bring me anything!"

"Maybe it fell under the bed," I mumbled groggily.

"Huh?" he asked. "Why would it be under the bed?"

"Just look," I told him.

He crawled over the side of the bed and looked underneath. "Nope, don't see anything," he said, climbing back beside me.

I sighed and turned over on my stomach, looking through the space between the mattress and headboard. "I'll bet it fell down here," I suggested.

Jason stretched out and peered down there, too. "I don't see anything."

I mustered all the energy I could at that hour of the morning. "Wait!" I exclaimed, "There's something right here!" I sounded genuinely surprised and excited, a great acting job. Then I reached down and grabbed the plastic baggie filled with quarters and, with a flourish, I handed it to Jason. His face dropped, obviously disappointed. He took the baggie between two fingers and held it up in the air, out and away from him, like it was a dirty diaper, staring at it.

"The Tooth Fairy left me *this?*" he asked. I started to remind him there are four quarters in a dollar so this was a lot of money, but I knew that coins in a bag couldn't hold a candle to a crisp $5 bill. Okay, I thought, perhaps the time really had come to tell him the truth. I took a deep breath and started to speak, when Jason suddenly grinned. "Hey I know," he said, "since it was a silver tooth, she wanted to bring me silver coins."

I looked at him, impressed by his explanation and a little disappointed in myself that I hadn't thought of it first. I can't think on my feet like I used to be able to do. I patted him on the back and said, "I'll bet that's it." Definitely, I'm getting too old for this Tooth Fairy gig.

I'm NOT the Grandma

When Jason was almost eight, he and I drove into a convenience store parking lot to get gas. "Mom, can we go in and get some candy corn?" he asked. He'd just had a terrific day at a summer basketball camp, and so I decided to reward him with his request. After pumping the gas, we walked into the store which was packed with construction workers obviously there for the Two Hot Dogs for a Buck lunch special. Since the place was so busy, they had two sales clerks to handle the rush, one behind each end of the counter. We got in the shortest line and waited. When we got to the counter to pay, the clerk, a large man probably in his 50s, started making small talk with Jason and asked him a math question about how much Jason would have to pay if he bought three bags of candy corn instead of one. Jason glanced at me with wide eyes as if to say 'boy, Mom this guy is really weird'.

But the store clerk took Jason's hesitation to mean he didn't know the answer to the question and was looking to me for help, so the man nodded toward me and said, "If you don't know, ask your grandma." I froze immediately as I was reaching for a pack of Mentos, and my horror-filled eyes met the clerk's who must have sensed he'd made a mistake. "Mom?" he asked, correcting himself. But it was too late. The damage had been done.

I forced a smile. "Yes, it's mom," I replied, trying not to call attention to myself or the situation.

"Okay, *mom* then," the clerk said and gave me back my change.

I hurried the heck out of there, and when we were outside Jason said, "Mom, you do know he just insulted you?" As the youngest of three boys, he is definitely good at recognizing a stinging insult when he hears one. Lord knows he and his brothers certainly trade insults enough.

"Yes, Jason, I know."

"Maybe he was just kidding," Jason offered. Bless his heart.

"No, I don't think he was kidding," I told Jason.

"Well then he was really rude," he replied. I opened the car door and contemplated for a moment those stories you see on the news sometimes about people who accidentally drive their cars through store windows. Hmmm ... a stuck accelerator sounded viable. I thought about it, but I resisted.

We drove along in silence, but I was reliving the convenience store episode in my mind all the way home. The man had called me Grandma. Of course, I looked forward to being a grandmother someday, but I didn't want to be mistaken for the grandmother of my own child. The thing was I'd thought I'd looked pretty good or at least decent that day; I had on make-up and clothes that matched and even had self-tanner on my legs. As the afternoon and evening went on, I replayed in my mind what the clerk had said and actually started wondering if perhaps he really had been kidding with me as Jason had suggested. Or maybe that was just wishful thinking on my part. He was the talkative type and maybe he was having a little fun, spicing up a rather boring day behind the store counter. I tried to recall the exact tone of his voice, the flicker of his eyes, to determine if he had been serious. And if he had been serious, what specifically was it about me that made him think I was Jason's grandma? I knew I could not wonder about that moment the rest of my life. I knew I had to find out. I had to go back.

The next day, the last day of Jason's basketball camp, I casually asked Jason when he got in the car if he'd like some more candy corn. "Sure!" he replied, surprised as to the cause of my sudden generosity but not about to question it.

So there we were again with another bag of candy corn amidst the construction workers who were buying hot dogs and burritos. I'd made sure to explain to Jason beforehand that he was not to say a single word to the clerk about what happened. Jason has always said what's on his mind, and it would have been just like him to go up to the guy and tell him what a moron he was. Part of me wanted Jason to say that to the man or even more so—wanted me to yell, "What kind of blankety-blank jackass calls a customer a grandmother unless he is sure she really is a grandma?" But of course I didn't say that.

I decided to buy a few more items so it wouldn't seem odd, like we had an addiction and had to make a candy corn run every day at noon. I grabbed a box of Kleenex, some Beef Jerky, and a road map. Strange combination, I know, but I had to work quickly so I got what was nearby. Jason took his bag of candy corn and started up to the counter, but he was headed to the other clerk's line. He was about to sabotage my whole plan. "Jason!" I shouted. "Over here!" I pulled him back down one of the aisles with me, waiting for our chance. I had to time our approach to the counter just right because there was now only one single line with the next person in line going to whatever clerk was free first, like at the bank. I had to make sure we got the right clerk.

Jason didn't understand what all the fuss was about as I gauged the timing of my mission. When the line dwindled and I could tell we would be the next customer, I hurried Jason into the line. We walked up to the clerk, and he looked at us with recognition in his eyes. I placed the items on the counter and he began to ring them up.

"Hello there again," he said.

"Hey," Jason replied stoically. Jason knew I was planning to say or do something to the man, but I hadn't told him what. By his quiet and nervous demeanor, I realized he might be expecting poor ole' Mom to pepper spray the guy.

The clerk smiled. "More candy corn, I see."

I nodded and jumped at the chance to respond. "Yes, but this time you don't have to ask if I'm his mom or his grandma." I smiled and waited for his response, hoping he'd grin and say he'd been teasing me.

He winced a bit. "Oh, I'm sorry about that," he apologized. Then he added, "But honey, you *had* to have had him late."

Say what? Okay, I think I'd rather be called a grandma. His words sunk in rapidly, and I hated the way he'd stressed that first 'had', like there was no doubt about it whatsoever. "Honey, you *had* to have had him late." Then anger began to well up inside of me, and I spoke back to him. "Well, I was 38. That's not young, but I wouldn't say it's late."

"Well, it's later than usual," he replied.

"Lots of women have babies way into their forties," I said.

"Yeah, but you weren't like 21."

"No, I wasn't 21, but most women who have babies these days aren't 21 either. That's actually pretty young." By this time the man knew he'd opened a can of worms, and I'm sure he was regretting ever uttering the word 'grandma' to me. "Besides," I went on, "in today's society with more women working, couples put off having kids until later, so 38 is not really out of the ordinary." I sounded like I was a guest on The View and half expected Whoopi Goldberg's voice to cut in and say, "We'll be right back with more hot topics."

The poor guy didn't know what hit him. "Well, I didn't mean 38 was old," he said, "it's just later in life than most people have babies."

I started to respond, but then I noticed Jason standing there innocently holding his bag of candy corn and looking back and forth between us as we debated like he was watching a tennis match. Okay, it was time to make peace.

"Hey, I understand what you meant, but it kind of came out wrong," I told him, getting my bag of items off the counter and walking toward the door.

As Jason and I were exiting, the clerk winked and shouted, "But you're still lookin' good!" As if that would appease me. Too little too late, buddy. I felt like calling all my friends and organizing a protest in front of the store. We could march in circles in the parking lot with picket signs, shouting, "Thirty-eight's not late! Some women want to wait!" Surely a 6:00 news story if I ever heard one. They could zoom in on the bag of candy corn with the overdramatic voiceover (aka William Shatner) saying, "All they wanted was a bag of candy, but what they got were age-related insults." Yet, I knew I couldn't take it that far. But I will definitely not be buying candy corn from that guy anymore. Boycott, ladies, boycott.

Age Spots & Diaper Rash

The appearance of age spots is one of the most frustrating parts of getting older for all women. These spots appear because of hormones and sun exposure and a bunch of other crap. Older moms are very prone to these because of the hormones of pregnancy and their lasting effects. What is really irritating is having to deal with age spots at the same time we are also buying diaper rash cream for our babies. Pigment lightening gel, fade cream, and A&D ointment used to sit side by side in my bathroom cabinet. There were probably a few times I got them mixed up and put fade cream on Jason's butt, but I don't notice that it hurt him any. But it's tough to have to worry about two such different skin problems at the same time.

Actually, I remember getting my very first brown spot on my face when I was a mere 25 years old. This has oddly and sadly become a memory of 'firsts': my first steps, my first date, my first car, my first age spot. I was on my honeymoon and had just recently started taking birth control pills. We flew into Palm Springs where we began our trip north up the California coastline. I'd been out by the pool relaxing in the desert sun, and when I came inside I caught a glimpse of me in the mirror and screamed. Literally screamed. For there on my forehead was a raggedy-edged brown spot, caused of course by the sun exposure (though I did have on sunscreen) and the unfamiliar effects of birth control pills. Kevin, being a brand new husband, claimed he didn't see anything, which, although he was trying to be nice, drove me up the wall because I knew the spot was there.

This was proven to me when I returned to work after the honeymoon. I was working in a radio station at the time, and the newly-hired sales clerk—a young, tan beauty with straight, non-frizzy blonde hair—was the object of desire for every man there. She wasn't the brightest but she was usually friendly, so the rest of the women at the station didn't hate her too badly. When I returned to work after my honeymoon, I was a bit self-conscious about the brown spot on my forehead. Kevin said I was overreacting and that nobody would notice. As the end of the day approached, I thought he might have been right because no one had said anything about it.

Alas, the final project of the day was to work on a sales proposal with the new sales clerk, Christie. As I went over the promotional elements of the project, I noticed she was staring at me—but not making eye contact—and I suddenly realized she was looking at my brown spot. Christie seemed to be mesmerized by it, as if it were casting some kind of spell on her, kind of like when a man is talking to a woman but the woman can tell he's really looking at her boobs. Yep, she was looking at my brown spot. I felt my face turn red but I went on talking, hoping the moment would pass. Then she interrupted, saying loudly, "Hey did you know you've got a big spot on your head?" with about as much tact as Rush Limbaugh at an Obama family reunion.

What could I say? "Yes, I know," I told her, trying my best to smile. "It's from the hormones in the birth control pill because my body isn't used to them." She looked at me quizzically, her head tilted sideways. The brown spot faded throughout the next year, but other spots gradually took its place. And more. And more. Still, I'll always have a special place in my heart for that first one.

I don't have to worry about diaper rash creams any more, but I do have to worry about Jason's eczema. We have plenty of creams and ointments for that, but there are still far more jars of age spot and wrinkle creams than anything else, due to the enormous amount of marketing that is done to make women feel inadequate if they are unable to escape the natural effects of time. The constant bombardment of anti-aging products targeted to women is overwhelming; there is no way women should have to do this much stuff to themselves as they get older. The list is never ending. With commercials and infomercials, advertisers pitch thousands of products to us poor women 24 hours a day. I can't turn on the TV without one of them coming on. Leave us the hell alone! We can't possibly find the time or money to fix all the stuff the TV spokesperson says is wrong with us. We have lives, people! Not only are we seduced by ads for smoother skin and weight loss, there are products out there that make our eyelashes longer, our hair voluminous, our nails perfect, our lips fuller, our stomachs less bloated, and our thighs with less cellulite. Why are women made to feel that every single part of their bodies has to be perfect?

Yet, I must admit—those infomercials for miracle skin products have a certain appeal. I'm extremely skeptical at the start of these infomercials, but if I don't turn the station fast enough, their outlandish claims and their celebrity spokespeople draw me right in, almost like they're hypnotizing me. The more I listen, the easier it is to believe that—yes—the secret to erasing wrinkles really *could* be the juice of a rare melon discovered in a southern region of France (an actual claim from a Cyndi Crawford skin product, and they make it sound *so* scientific).

Since Jason experienced a lot of eczema when he was a baby, I also went on-line and was seduced by a lot of ads there for miracle creams that would magically make all of his skin problems go away. Sure, I ordered a few until I had to finally admit that there was no such thing as a miracle cream. Over time the eczema gradually got better, but it has been a long road that has included a plethora of prescription ointments, over the counter products, and off the wall 'remedies' like blue emu cream.

Even though I know better, the allure of the infomercials and the promise of a possible miracle cream, still persuade me from time to time. In a weak moment when the remote was out of reach and my credit card was nearby, there was once when I ordered one of those "Face Lift in a Jar" type products that smooth out all facial wrinkles for 24 hours (if you can't be wrinkle-free permanently, I'll settle for temporarily especially for class reunions). As I listened to the Face Lift infomercial, I became more gullible by the minute. Soon I was grabbing for a pencil to write down the 1-800 number. "Call in the next ten minutes and receive free eye cream as our gift," the TV announcer continued. As if I needed more persuasion.

When the UPS guy dropped it off, I grabbed it before my husband saw it and ran upstairs behind closed doors to try this miracle product in secret. I wanted to make sure I applied the cream correctly because I didn't want the skin on my face to get so tight that it cracked. But when I unfolded the instructions, the print was too damn small to read! If a woman is old enough to spend money on face lift creams, then she's too old to read tiny print. What were they thinking? Large print is definitely the way to go here. I looked on the Internet to see the product's reviews, and some women said they'd tried it, only to have people ask them, "What is wrong with your face?" Not quite the effect I was hoping it to have. I put the jar in the bathroom cabinet, and there it still sits.

But I know that creams and ointments are the only things I'll probably ever use to fight the effects of aging because plastic surgery and Botox are just too expensive and risky. Some people might say those things are vain, but I think it is more of a matter of self-confidence than vanity, especially as we get older. Still, I'm afraid I'd be plagued with guilt if I took money we might need in the future for something really important and spend it on a skin procedure. Yet, don't moms deserve to spend something on themselves sometime? If we can pay for a camper or season hockey tickets, what's wrong with spending money on something for me? I hear similar quandaries from women my age all the time. Moms are used to putting themselves last, and so it's difficult to do otherwise.

Over the years, I've taught writing courses in elementary schools and even worked as a Teacher Assistant (where lunch duty and doing two digit multiplication the 'rectangle way' just about got the best of me). Children in elementary school are at that age where they say what they feel; their honesty can be refreshing and it can be brutal, especially to women in their 40s and 50s whose egos might be just a tad fragile. But I've discovered one thing that helps—no cure by any means—but sometimes it works: the power of distraction. If I'm having a particularly bad hair day or didn't get enough sleep the night before and have bags under my eyes, I make it a point to wear large jewelry.

Bright necklaces or earrings that detract the kids, so they comment on the jewelry instead of the way I look.

But it is tempting to have a 'procedure', and I would think in a family as big as mine there should be at least one plastic surgeon in all those cousins, aunts, and uncles, but sadly, there is not a single one. I've taken my sons to the dermatologist, and while waiting in the doctor's office, I've seen the brochures—you know the ones I'm talking about: the oh-so-tempting face lift and Botox color brochures with before and after pics— placed strategically to catch mom's attention while she's waiting with her kids. And then there's Juvederm and Fraxel, two words that women will become familiar with as they get older because they will Google them so often but most will never take action. FYI for those who have not yet hit this point of desperation: Juvederm is a gel filler specifically for those wrinkles around the nose and mouth, while Fraxel is a laser treatment that reduces wrinkles and age spots on the entire face. The brochures in the dermatologist's office on these are especially enticing.

Once, I even asked out of curiosity how much the procedures cost, but I know more than likely I'll never actually have one done. Money you might want to spend on things like Botox goes instead to bunion or gall stone surgery. You see, just when you're old enough to need cosmetic surgery, the stuff that enables you to do basic things like walk and digest food begins to deteriorate, and you have to spend your hard-earned cash for that. It's like Mother Nature is laughing at you all the way to the bank.

Since we're older moms, the money will probably go instead to pay for our child's braces, math tutor, or college accounts. Or to eczema and diaper rash creams.

Definitely more important than cosmetic procedures for me. I'll just accept those age spots and wrinkles as badges of honor, despite what the commercials say. But if I ever win the lottery, I will call Juvederms 'R Us so fast it'll make your head spin.

Attempted Advice
to My College Son

When my oldest son, Billy, moved into his North Carolina State University dorm room in the fall of 2009, his roommate's mom and I found ourselves in the odd role of being a visitor in our son's room. We wanted to stay and help organize things, but yet it became clear that the guys wanted us to leave: this was their own turf now. No matter how cool you ever were before at home, no parents—or their advice—are cool at college. And a parent has to realize that like it or not—time has gone by since we ourselves were in college.

One mistake I made was buying an erasable memo board for Billy to hang outside his door. He pulled it out of the bag and asked, "What's this for?"

"When I was in college," I explained, my voice filled with the wisdom of experience, "everybody had memo boards on their door so if someone came by and you weren't there, then they could write a message that they had stopped by." I looked over at Billy and realized he was trying to politely suppress his laughter. I was obviously a source of amusement for my child. "What?" I asked, defensively.

"Mom," he said, smiling broadly, "now we just text each other."

"Yeah, but," I started to reply and then stopped, knowing I had no response. Okay, I admit there had been some advances in technology in almost thirty years. "Well, it was always exciting to come back and see if you had a message on your door," I told him, defiantly. "You're missing out."

"Do you still have the receipt?" he asked, still grinning.

Yet another mistake I made was on the third day he was there and I'd just dropped off some more merchandise from Bed, Bath, & Beyond (by the way, it's so obvious at these stores which moms have daughters leaving for college and which ones have sons. The ones with daughters actually have their daughters shopping *with them* and they are discussing comforter colors and room décor details, while the ones with sons are by themselves with forlorn expressions and are just buying the bare necessities like towels and a laundry bag.) Anyway, as Billy was impatiently waiting for me to leave the dorm, I went to the laundry room to see if the washer only took quarters or if it would accept his ATM card. I discovered it would only take quarters or the special all campus card, but *not* ATM cards.

I attempted to share this information with my son, but he cut me off with an "Okay, Mom" and an exasperated glance. I offered him some quarters, but the look got more exasperated. It was time for me to leave. It's painful to realize you are being brushed off by your adult child, the same person who used to be your little boy who'd cling to every word you said and give you hugs and looks of admiration. Even though this was all part of the 'letting go' process, I was so glad Jason still gave me hugs.

A few days later, my husband happened to call Billy, who at the time was walking downtown to get quarters since the laundry room wouldn't take his ATM card; his dormitory office and the student store had no quarters left, due to high student demand for them. There he was scouring campus for quarters, surely regretting that he'd disregarded good ole Mom's advice. Ah, sweet validation.

The Thanksgiving Cake

As a woman ages, her priorities somehow change, too. With mothers, these priorities usually involve her kids. This first became obvious to me on Thanksgiving years ago when my two oldest sons were in elementary school. My father's side of the family always meets in Fayetteville, North Carolina, a city about an hour away from my home, on Thanksgiving for a family get-together. He comes from a family of 12 children so you can imagine how many people are there.

This is the one time a year that I see all these relatives, so I've always tried to make a good impression—or at least not a bad one. I used to always wear a new sweater and even attempt to style my hair so it wouldn't frizz so much. I noticed the relatives of my generation made this same effort to look their best for this annual 'scrutiny of the relatives'. Except for an easy casserole, my cousins and I left the cooking to the older generation—our moms. They are the ones who baked the homemade from-scratch cakes and added secret ingredients to the delicious potato salad.

But that particular year I decided to make a homemade carrot cake with cream cheese frosting just like my mother made a few times before, but it wasn't one of her signature ones like pineapple and coconut. She hadn't made it quite a while, and I missed it. So the night before Thanksgiving, I grated carrot after carrot, realizing I never thanked Mama nearly enough for all the stuff she'd cooked over the years. I eventually got all three layers out of the cake pans, but one of them stuck, ripping out a chunk of cake. I pieced it back together like a jigsaw puzzle and discovered if I positioned the cake just right, nobody could tell.

By the time I was ready to make the frosting, it was past eleven. I plodded on, determined. The frosting, however, did not cooperate, looking too thin and runny. The cake looked nowhere near like Mama's. Or for that matter like any other cake I'd ever seen. I decided the only thing to do was to get up the next morning and make a second recipe of frosting.

So on Thanksgiving Day, I began my baking in earnest once more. The second recipe did the trick, covering the three layers with thick, swirled frosting. I still had to chop the nuts and put them on the top and sides of the cake. I checked my watch. We were running late. If we were going to get to Fayetteville on time, then I knew I had to make a choice: I could either spend the time getting myself ready or perfecting my cake.

And this is where I knew I was getting older: I chose the cake. Instead of putting on a nice outfit and getting jewelry to accessorize—instead of using a curling iron on my hair—I threw on an old pair of jeans and got my cake ready to go. A new generation had arrived. The torch had been passed. I was now one of the women at the Thanksgiving dinner who cared more about how their food was accepted than what anyone thought about the way they looked. I mentioned this to a friend of mine who suggested perhaps this new perspective means we're now more comfortable with ourselves—more confident in who we are—and that we don't base our identity so much on how we look. And indeed this might be part of it. But the other part is, of course, as we get older, we see ourselves in different roles. My 'mom' role was coming through loud and clear.

No, it's not about who makes the best pies or cakes; it's about creating heartwarming memories of family gatherings—times to be recalled fondly by our children years from now, so vividly they can remember how the sweet potato pie tasted or the wonderful aroma of turkey filling the house.

The carrot cake was quite a success with only a few crumbs left on the plate. As a cousin complimented me on it and asked for the recipe, I smiled, shrugged my shoulders, and lied through my teeth, "Oh, it's pretty easy to make." I've taken the cake to the get-together every year since then and make it for a few other holidays too. My sons all like it, so I feel that it's something special I can make that they truly appreciate. I like to make this cake every now and then when David comes home from college for a weekend or Billy stops by the house after work. It feels good for them to be home. And then I say, "There's a carrot cake on the counter," and I hope that makes home even more special to them.

Thanksgiving morning is still hectic at my house. Our dog is usually barking, and my husband is singing "Over the River and Through the Woods" in a loud, off-key voice just to annoy my sons. I'm usually scurrying around trying to find some clothes for me that don't have to be ironed and begging my sons to shave. If I'm lucky, I might find time to actually put on eyeliner and wrinkle cream. But my number one priority is still the cake.

In the Trenches on Field Day

Ahhhh ... field day—that elementary school tradition where kids go outside and play games in the sunshine. The sack race, the bean bag toss, maybe a moon bounce, and sometimes water games to keep the kids cool in the heat. Such was the scene at Jason's elementary school when he was in kindergarten. I remembered the field days my two older sons had, but since there is a pretty big age gap between them and Jason, it'd been a while since I'd volunteered for the event. But I decided to volunteer for Jason's field day despite the weather forecast calling for 94 degree heat. I got my water bottle and sunscreen and headed out to the school, oblivious to the fact that it had been almost five years since I'd attempted this feat before. This, I failed to realize, meant I was now five years older than I was then. And let me tell ya, that makes a big difference.

When I arrived, I got my assigned activity: the Ball Throw, which consisted of kids trying to knock over sand-filled plastic bottles with Wiffle® balls. Sounded easy enough. I walked down to the field and met another parent volunteer, a dad of a second-grader, who was assigned to work with me at the Ball Throw. There were two lines set up with three Wiffle® balls for each line; one line used purple balls and one line used yellow ones. The instruction sheet for our game simply said we were to make sure the kids stood behind the pink cone when they threw and to set up the bottles again after they fell. Hey, I could that. Yet, the other parent volunteer and I soon realized there was more to this than meets the eye. Whenever the balls missed the bottles (which was most of the time), they would sail way down the field. And somebody—probably the parent volunteers I'd say—had to retrieve them. This was okay for the first 15 minutes or so. But as we chased the balls all over the field time after time in the scorching hot sun, the other parent and I soon realized we were both about to pass out. At first it was comical, as we made jokes about getting exercise. Then we started devising plans to have the children retrieve their own balls. The first thing we attempted was to tell the child in line behind the child throwing the balls that he/she had to retrieve the balls before he/she could throw. It didn't work because they ended up trying to throw them back in, and we were being pelted by Wiffle® balls.

We pointed to the other games and tried to interest the kids in them more than ours by shouting things like, "Wow, that sack race looks like a lot of fun!" Only an hour had passed, and it had passed very slowly, I might add. Purple and yellow Wiffle® balls were flying all over the place. Trying to explain the rules to kids who don't really listen took more energy than we had left. We looked longingly at the parents volunteering at the water games, getting doused with a cool spray of water every now and then. We were envious of the lady standing in the middle of the field with foam swimming pool noodles and no kids in line. The object of the game was to throw the noodle, but nobody seemed interested. My volunteer partner—I think his name was Joe—but we were both so delirious from the heat and exhaustion I'm not really sure—went over and asked her what the name of her game was. "The Snake Pass," she told him. I'm sure she was bored but at least she was not panting for breath or getting her legs bruised by errant Wiffle® balls. 'Joe' came back over and said, "The Snake Pass—that's what we sign up for next year." I committed the name to memory, although I decided I'd rather go for those water games next year myself. Did I say next year??? We really were delirious.

Finally, we hit on something that worked. We just firmly told the kids that once they threw the balls, they had to go get them. Each one of them seemed okay with that until their first throw when they'd see it sail down the field 50 yards away. Their little faces would look distraught and they'd look at us, expecting us to go get it for them. Being much smarter this time around, 'Joe' and I would smile and say "Go get it!" like that was half the fun. This worked for most of the rest of the afternoon, although there was that one time a teacher came over to watch and doing the instinctive thing, he ran out to retrieve a ball. "NO!!" 'Joe' and I both yelled at the same time as we held up our hands to signal him to stop. The teacher looked at us, startled—and maybe a little taken aback by our passionate plea.

Joe explained—perhaps a little too vehemently, "If they see you doing that, they won't retrieve their own balls. It'll mess up the whole system." The teacher dropped the Wiffle® ball back on the ground like he was Superman getting rid of kryptonite, looking at us suspiciously and backing cautiously away. Clearly a novice.

When field day was finally over, Joe and I said good-bye, and I felt a kind of comradeship with him. We'd been through the field day trenches together; we had faced the challenge, and neither one of us had passed out from heat exhaustion. We congratulated each other on not having to call EMS to resuscitate us (totally serious here). And we had a few suggestions for the instructions for next year's Ball Throw.

As I got in my SUV, I sucked down a bottle of water, cranked the air conditioner up high, and picked up my cell phone. I dialed a friend of mine from our local moms of boys group who had recently had her third boy a decade after her first. When she answered the phone, I said in a worn-out voice, "When your youngest gets in kindergarten, whatever you do, don't volunteer for field day." I felt it was my duty to warn her. She didn't quite understand it then, but she will. ... she will.

Another Awkward Moment

As my own children grow up and leave the nest one by one, I sometimes long to hold a baby in my arms again. I know a lot of women with older children feel the same way. Fortunately for me, my niece Kristin had a beautiful baby girl in 2009 and a baby boy in 2013. Jason, who was eight when the little girl was born, was especially eager for the baby to arrive. Years earlier when he was four, Jason told me one night he'd made a wish on a star that he would have a little sister. "Ah, sweetheart," I said, breaking the news to him as gently as I could, "that isn't going to happen." I almost added, "Not a snowball's chance in hell," but I caught myself.

Kristin and Jason are cousins, but there is a twenty year age gap in between them. When we first found out Kristin was expecting, I was assisting two other adults in teaching Jason's Sunday School class when one of the adults asked students to share something that had happened to them during the past week. Jason's hand shot up immediately, a huge grin appearing on his face, barely able to contain his enthusiasm. He even made a few of those 'ooh-ooh' noises Arnold Horshack used to make on Welcome Back Kotter. "Yes, Jason?" one of the adults responded, smiling, probably expecting a story about a soccer or basketball team victory or a trip to Disney.

"My cousin is pregnant!" Jason shouted. The other two teachers didn't know quite how to respond. The thing is—people usually assume that an 8-year-old has cousins near his own age or maybe in their teens, and they had obviously made this assumption. They looked awkwardly at me, their eyes wide. "Yes," I replied quickly, "my niece and her *husband* announced last weekend they are expecting a baby in November." I emphasized the word 'husband' to get my point across. They breathed a sigh of relief that Jason hadn't spilled the beans about a delicate family situation.

Yet another awkward moment of being an older mom. Will they never end?

Looking Good for Childbirth?

I happened to come across a recent article in *The Boston Globe* about how many moms-to-be plan to look good for their immediate post-childbirth photos. Damn, I thought labor was my one time to have a really good excuse to look like crap and not worry about it. Don't take that away from me! Yet, there it was in black and white: "Thanks to Facebook and Twitter, giving birth has become a much more public event. Some new moms are primping on the big day." Primping? Seriously? I understand a mom's desire to look halfway decent in photos with her newborn child, but to actually orchestrate it all with manicures, pedicures, and hair styling before and even during labor? Sure, I took some mascara and lipstick with me to apply before I left the hospital, but during labor and immediately after, the way I looked was not what was on my mind.

When I had my oldest son, I was in the hospital in labor for 13 hours, including 2 and a half hours of doing nothing but PUSHING. This all happened from 8 pm until 9 a.m., meaning I lost an entire night's sleep in addition to enduring the most awful pain I'd ever experienced (with the exception of when my arm fat gets caught in the automatic car door lock when my arm is propped by the window). I was exhausted emotionally, physically, and mentally. The photos taken right after my son's birth are evidence of my hard work: dark circles under my eyes, hair a mess, one of those cute hospital gowns having come untied on my shoulder. Sexy, I'm sure. The word 'episiotomy' had just become exceedingly real to me—I had an 8 and a half pound baby boy I was trying to teach to 'latch on' so I could attempt to breastfeed him, and I was so tired I couldn't lift my head off the pillow. I didn't care how I looked at that moment, and I didn't mind photos capturing the reality of it all; later the next day, I did put on a bit of make-up for a family photo, but that was it. Ditto and Ditto again for sons 2 and 3. I can't imagine having to plan my wardrobe and hair appointments in addition to getting ready for a new baby. I understand if some women chose to do this, but I don't want it to become an expectation, the rule instead of the exception. Quite frankly, I think giving birth is enough of an accomplishment for one day—I'll save looking my best for another day, thank you very much.

And a quote in the article I found interesting was from style blogger Roxanna Sarmiento, mother of three: "But those after childbirth pictures last forever. Anyone can see them five or 10 years from now. Even future employers." Okay, let me just say for the record that if a potential employer decided not to hire me because I didn't look beautiful and well-coiffed after just going through labor, then I really, really, wouldn't want to work there in the first place. Is this what the world is coming to? Employers can add your childbirth photos to your application file with your resume and references? "You were the leading candidate for the job, but then we saw your Facebook childbirth photos, and your hair looked like crap, so I'm sorry we'll have to go with someone else."

Don't fall for it, ladies. Don't give into the demands to look good while pushing another human being out of your body. They don't call it labor for nothing.

Trying to Be Social Media Savvy

I've tried to be a cool mom who understands all the technology and social media that teens use; but, as soon as you master Facebook, they've moved on to Twitter, and as soon as you've mastered that, they've moved on to Instagram, SnapChat, etc. For the life of me, I don't understand why you want to send someone a picture that disappears like it does on Snapchat. Heck, when a photo pops up on my phone, I have to either remember how to enlarge it or find my glasses to see it well, and by that time, it'd be gone.

Unfortunately, sometimes moms know just enough about social media to gain access to their kids' posts, feeds, Tweets, and friends list but not enough to remember the differences between the various social media. In Facebook, you just tap a photo and then enlarge it by widening it with your fingers; yet, on Instagram, if you tap on a photo, surprise! You have just officially 'liked' the photo although you didn't intend to do so, especially since you are stalking the account of a prospective boyfriend or girlfriend of your kid. Even on Facebook where I usually feel comfortable, if I go on the page of somebody one of my sons has just started dating to find out more about her (because let's face it, boys don't share details with moms), I am nervous about inadvertently hitting the 'like' button, alerting her to the fact I've been snooping. Trust me, I know other moms have this same fear. When I go on 'her' page, I'm saying to myself the whole time, "Don't click the like button, don't click the like button." I've found this is especially perilous if I'm on my phone instead of the actual computer; I've made it a point to snoop only when I'm on my computer where there is less of a chance of my clumsy fingers mistakenly hitting anything I don't intend to hit.

I even have problems with things when they are on my sons' phones. There have been times one of them will want me to see a photo on their Instagram account, and so they hold their phone out for me to look. On instinct, I immediately try to enlarge the photo by tapping on it as I do on Facebook, eliciting screams of "Mom, no!" from my sons. I just think it would make a lot of sense if these social media outlets would simply get on the same page with this stuff and make basic things the same. Tapping a photo should have the same results regardless of what social medium you are using. Moms everywhere would thank them.

Texting is awesome for parents, even though, yes, we have to make sure everyone understands the dire danger of texting while driving. Texting makes communicating so much easier. I remember when I first started texting, and it was incredible to go pick up a son somewhere and simply text "I'm here" and he would come right to the car. No having to get out and go to the door, no phone calls that my son didn't answer, no having to run into people when I had no make-up on, no hassle. Teens often don't want to get involved in conversation (don't want to interrupt watching Netflix!), but they can text quickly. We have a family group text that certainly makes our communication easier and ensures that we all get the same info about the times and places of events. Still, most of our group texts involve sports, such as game commentary and recruiting news. Once I was about to enter a funeral service, and all of a sudden my phone started buzzing in my purse. One buzz after another. I immediately knew there must be something going on in the sports world and that all my boys were texting in our family group text. Either a trade the Red Sox just made or a recruit that North Carolina State just signed. So I stopped at the back of the church and switched off my phone, glimpsing the big news that State had indeed signed a top basketball recruit. I was happy about that news, too, but dang it they *knew* I was at a funeral right then.

A few years ago, one of my nephews showed me how to take a photo of a screen shot of a text. Several days later while sitting in my car in a parking lot, I decided to use my newfound knowledge. While waiting in the car for my youngest son, I was listening to a radio sports talk show and was interested in their analysts' comments about a college basketball game the previous night. The game involved my college sons' university, North Carolina State and its rival, the University of North Carolina at Chapel Hill. Before this big game, David, my middle son, had texted to our family text that the key match-up in the game would be that of Justin Jackson for UNC and Maverick Rowan for NC State because Rowan would have a hard time guarding the quicker Jackson. It turned out to be prophetic. NC State came out and took a big lead until yes—Jackson went on a scoring streak , helping the UNC Tar Heels win. The next day on the sports radio show, the announcers were talking about how the tide of the game had turned when Jackson went on that scoring spree and how the match-up between him and Rowan was a terrible one. Why was Rowan ever matched up to guard Jackson, they asked.

Of course, this same sports insight was said BEFORE the game by my son, so as I sat there in my car listening to the sports show, I decided hey—I'll take a screen shot of the text from my son and send it to the sports show via Twitter so that they can see how insightful my son was. And I did! I was so proud of myself for doing the screen shot and getting it to the show's hosts. What a savvy mom I was thinking. So what if I'm 53? I can handle all that technology stuff and follow sports as well as any 25-year-old. Right?

My phone buzzed within a minute of sending the Tweet. I looked and saw I had a Tweet from one of the show's hosts! No doubt they were going to comment on how insightful my son had been about that game match-up, how prophetic it was. They would also be impressed that I—an older mom—tweeted them a screen shot. Then I read the Tweet from the show's host: "Oh my goodness, look at that font size!" That was all it said. I was crushed and embarrassed. I guess the font is bigger than average, but I didn't think it was comment-worthy. He said nothing at all about the content of my son's text, nothing at all. I was so disappointed and was irritated with the show's host. To add insult to injury, I saw on Twitter, that my oldest son, Billy, had liked the host's response to my Tweet. Thanks, son.

Now we have ventured into the world of GIFs and memes. GIFs are brief clips of movies, shows, or other video that people use to respond about current events or peoples' comments. They are often sarcastic and funny. Memes are images used for the same purpose. I think some of these are quite humorous, but I also think that they, particularly the GIFs, can be an invasion of privacy.

Some poor girl cries when her team loses on TV and suddenly her crying fit is plastered all over social media and used in comments about other topics that involve overly-emotional people.

And don't even get started about the actual photos that we take with our phones and then post on social media. I'm not one for taking lots of photos of every event in my life or every place I go. I just want to live and enjoy the moment. One time in San Diego, we took a boat tour out in the harbor, and many of the people on the tour with us were so adamant about getting selfies that they spent all their time posing instead of enjoying the scenery. And a few times they were even blocking the views of others. There is such a thing as taking a good thing to an extreme.

I see so many photos on social media in which the females stand slightly turned with their hand on their hip. That is said to be the most flattering stance. But it is not natural for me to stand that way. It's just not me. Some moms look great posing that way, but I just can't bring myself to do it. Maybe I don't have enough confidence in myself or something, but I simply don't feel comfortable standing like that.

But the thing that I hate most about social media photos is being tagged in a photo. This means that someone who took a photo of you somewhere has posted the photo on Facebook and has labeled your photo with your name so that the photo pops up on your Facebook page as well as the page of the person who posts the photo. If this is a posed photo, then at least you were aware it was taken and it is not a complete surprise. But a candid shot can be a problem—like the ones when you are photographed with your eyes closed or your mouth open or you looking down, which accents your double chin, or in the case of one wedding—me in the midst of dancing, and I'm not quite sure what dance move I was doing at the time, but it was not exactly flattering. These candid ones are the ones that pop up on your Facebook page after you are tagged in them, and you see it and say, "Oh, shit."

I actually sent a note to someone once that read: "That was a wonderful party last night. Everybody really enjoyed it! Do you think you could untag me in the photos you posted?" It's not about being vain; it's about trying not to be embarrassed. I wouldn't mind if my close friends see it, but I'm Facebook friends with more than just close friends, such as business acquaintances and yes, even a few guys I used to date. Post your photo on your page if you want, but please don't tag me in it and have it show up front and center on my page. (Update: my teenager recently showed me a setting on Facebook that allows me to pre-approve tagged photos. Glory be! Wish I had discovered this well-kept secret years ago.)

If it's a group photo, it's not nearly so bad because they are not as close-up, and you are not the only thing in the picture. One time I was at a bridal shower for a friend's daughter, and quite a lot of the women there were her daughter's age. They played a game in which we divided into groups and were given toilet paper rolls from which to design and make a toilet paper wedding dress. Each group had a 'model' who wore the toilet paper draped around them, while the others worked to cut and tie the paper to make it look like an actual dress. Making such a dress is a craft to me, and I am no good at crafts, which everyone knows. Thus, I reluctantly agreed to be the model for my group. At the end of the event, the models from all five groups of women went to the front of the room where we all stood in our just-made toilet paper dresses. That's when I realized that all the other models were around 22 years old. And then there was me—just a slight 30-year age gap between me and the other bride models.

Later when I got home, I went in to check my email messages and take a quick look at my Facebook page. I discovered that horror of horrors—I had been TAGGED. Oh God, I thought, this can't be good. And then I remembered while all of us toilet paper brides had been posing at the end of the game, there had been an inordinate amount of flash photography as women held up their cameras in a little group. A veritable horde of photographers.

Then I saw the photo, and I thanked God it wasn't a close-up. But I did post below the photo on Facebook the following: I did not know when I agreed to be a toilet paper model that there would be paparazzi. There are also certain unwritten laws about tagging. One of these is that if you are on vacation on the beach with no make-up on, then tagging is a no-no. This occurred when one of my nephews took a photo of my sisters and me on the beach, and none of us had make up on and our hair was blowing—and frizzing—in the wind. When we asked my nephew to take that particular photo down, he was confused. "But that's what you look like," he said. Yes, we know that's what we look like. That is the issue at hand. But we were relaxing, not trying to look our best. And yes, it is somewhat posed and yes, we knew he was taking it. But this is the kind of photo that the family sees and then maybe it would go in a drawer somewhere; it is not the kind of photo to post on Facebook—at least not when you are over 45. There is a definite line you don't cross, folks. A definite line.

II
The Caboose Baby

*Just as the caboose completes the train,
the caboose baby completes the family."*

—Sharon O'Donnell

The Age Gap Between Kids

(Shoot me now)

The nine year age gap between the oldest of my three sons and the youngest has definitely presented some interesting challenges. Having the third one has been different because he is more independent and learns things from his older brothers. It is also different for me because, well—I'm older the third time. The late night hours and early morning 'off to school' hours I've had to keep with the third one has had more of a physical effect on me than they did with the other boys. Sleep deprivation has been a lot more of an issue the third time around, from getting up in the night with him as a baby to waiting up now for him—a new driver—to get home.

There's also an element of sheer exhaustion that sets in at some point too, I must admit. Getting uptight about things and doling out discipline takes energy, and older parents sometimes run a little low on that.

The first day of kindergarten for each of my sons was an important day, but Jason was more independent than his brothers had been at that age so I didn't worry about him as much. With my older sons, I'd made sure they had the perfect breakfast and that they were feeling okay physically and emotionally. But the morning of

Jason's first day, Jason, who is prone to allergies, started coughing and even threw up once. I alarmed even myself by standing beside him at the toilet and simply looking at my watch and asking him, "Are you done? We have to hurry." Of course, I got emotional later, but right then I had my eye on the clock like I'd done so many years getting the other two out the door to school.

Being an older mom in certain situations with a younger child (particularly a world-savvy, sometimes sarcastic boy like Jason) requires a certain je ne sais quoi, an attitude that allows you to levy the appropriate punishment while at the same time knowing that this instance is a mere eye blink in time and that it will work out okay. An older mom has a different perspective than does a younger one. It's easier to see the big picture for us, and we know that just because we forget to take the cupcakes to the school carnival, the world will not end.

The main thing about being an older mom with age gap children is that I've already been there and done that, so to speak, and sometimes it's tough to go back. Re-adjusting to elementary school traditions can be especially hard for those moms who've gone on to middle and high school. For the love of God, do you know how much I dreaded writing Valentines for all the kids in the class and making a shoebox for Jason's mailbox? This is a craft to me, and craft is a four-letter word in my book. How many years must I do this? Is there not some type of maximum on parental torture? And I loved reading to Jason and his friends during lunch time at school each week, but how many more times could I read Dr. Seuss books aloud before I was officially declared out of my mind?

And there were those field trips where I had to make conversation with the moms of the other kids, who while very nice, were all probably a decade younger than I was. There I'd stand at age 47 at the third grade class picnic and listen politely as they talked about going to their 20th high school reunion or how their mother just turned 60. As I'd listen, my mind would automatically do the math and figure out an estimate of how much younger than me the other mom was.

Then there are the birthday parties. When Billy was little, I remember planning in great detail a Scooby-Do birthday party, when Scooby-Do merchandise was still incredibly difficult to find, so I had to scrounge to find Scooby stuff or make my own. I even had individual treasure chests filled with goodies hidden in the back yard with Scooby clues to help the kids solve the mystery and find the treasure. Was I nuts or what? And did I mention that Billy's birthday is in July so we were all searching for clues and treasure in 95 degree heat? It was different with Jason. I'd simply say, "Jason, do you want to have your party at Grand Slam baseball or the skating rink?" and then book the place pronto.

This age gap also means homework at our house has included everything from calculus for my oldest son, algebra for my middle one, to simple number sentences for my youngest. One night in the middle of all the homework hassles, Kevin and I were discussing what tutor to get for our oldest because helping him with his calculus was like Mission Impossible for us. Kevin understood it, but conveying the concepts to Billy was another story. That same night, my middle son brought home a test that wasn't up to his usual standards, and so Kevin was going over that with him, while I silently prayed to let us make it through until everybody's graduation. All the while in the back of my mind, I was panicking about all the years of homework to go with my youngest son, thinking, "We haven't even gotten to multiplication tables with Jason yet." It was an overwhelming thought, as I buried my head in my hands. We'd traveled down lots of roads with our older boys, but the journey was just beginning with Jason.

As parents, Kevin and I would sometimes forget Jason's young age and incorrectly assume he could do the same things our other guys were doing. This is a side effect of being older parents. One time when Jason was six and it was time for him to get dressed for ice hockey lessons, Kevin told him to do it himself. My dear husband obviously forgot how difficult it is to get all that equipment on, particularly if you're only six years old. "You've got to help him, Kevin," I reminded him. Of course, after all the gear was on—shoulder pads, chest pad, the hockey girdle, the thick socks snapped to the girdle—Jason said he had to go to the bathroom.

"Didn't you ask him if he had to pee before he got all that stuff on?" I asked Kevin. Mothers know that when that much equipment is involved, you always ask if they have to go to the bathroom beforehand. Indeed, he was used to dealing with the older guys.

For a few years, we had sons in high school, middle school, and elementary school, and with all those varying start times, our morning routine lasted from 5:15 a.m. when Billy woke up to catch the bus until 9:00 when I finally dropped Jason off in carpool. With one event after another in the mornings, sometimes my goal in life was simply not to be the last car in the carpool line.

When Jason was in fifth grade and brought home his form for me to sign up to volunteer at the school book fair, I got a pen and started to write my name. I stopped in mid-pen stroke as it dawned on me that this would be—wait for it—the last book fair I would ever have to volunteer for again. Whoa. I'd been volunteering for book fairs every year since my oldest was in kindergarten back in 1996; I don't really feel like doing the math right now, but that's a lot of book fairs, my friend. I'm surprised I didn't suffer from withdrawal symptoms or something. But realizing this would be my last one was bittersweet: none of my kids would be in elementary school any longer. My heart would always ache just a bit when I was in the carpool line to pick up my youngest, and I could so clearly imagine Billy and David standing side by side with their Pokeman backpacks, waiting for me the way they had years earlier. And if I were to go back to that school today, I would feel the same way reminiscing about how I used to pick up Jason. Memories of all three of them are all around that school, and I know I couldn't walk back in there or even drive into the parking lot without getting sentimental. I even saved the car tag with my carpool number on it—the one from Jason's last year in elementary school that would be my last carpool number ever. Sick, I know.

Even though I picked up my boys from school some in the afternoon, they also rode the bus a fair amount of time, too. There was once when it was pouring rain, and I was picking up Jason for the first time in about a month— only I was driving my husband's car that didn't have the car tag in it hanging from the mirror. This number is used so that a carpool helper can spot the number on our windshield and then say the number into a walkie— talkie, and that message is relayed to someone inside the school who will send out the child who corresponds to that number. Smooth process, right? Since my husband's car didn't have the carpool number, I'd have to tell the number to the carpool helper—an overworked, soaking wet staff member—when he or she came to my window.

But I had a brief memory lapse and couldn't remember my carpool tag number. I was pretty sure it was 471, but it was possible it was 417. Or maybe it was 741? When I rolled the window down to give the carpool helper the tag number, I told him 471.

It was still pouring as I inched my car closer to the front of the line; then I noticed there were other kids lined up in their called positions so that they would get into the appropriate car at the curb of the sidewalk. But Jason was nowhere in sight. I drove past the other kids standing in the rain with a few teachers trying to provide cover with some umbrellas. I stopped at the end of the sidewalk, and a carpool helper came to the window. I told her my son wasn't outside waiting for me, and I gave her Jason's name. I realized then that I must have told them the wrong carpool number. While I was waiting for them to bring Jason out, I turned and looked back at the kids in line for the cars and saw one little girl with pigtails who had been standing there since before I drove past. No car was stopping to pick her up. Then I realized who she was. She was number 471. And she was getting drenched by the rain because of me.

My passenger side door opened, and Jason got in. "Did you forget the carpool number, Mom?" he asked.

"I'm afraid I did. What is it?"

"741."

I shook my head, "Oh man, I got the first two numbers reversed." Before I pulled into the flow of traffic again, I glanced at the kids on the sidewalk. Poor little 471. I felt so guilty. I hoped her ride would be there soon. Usually, though, the carpool line went smoothly—a thing of orchestrated, perfectly timed beauty.

In addition to school volunteer events and seemingly endless carpool lines, Scouting activities were another thing that lasted forever since there was a nine year age gap between my youngest and oldest (actually a ten year gap in school years between Jason and Billy because Jason started a year late due to a late birthday). All three boys were in Tiger Scouts beginning in first grade, then Cub Scouts, and then Boy Scouts, with all three of them attaining the rank of Eagle Scout. That is indeed something to be proud of, but that also meant that our family had been to a lot of Scouting events over the years, including the regular Tuesday night meetings. Every Tuesday night from 1996 until 2017, one or more of our boys had a Scout meeting. That is a lot of Tuesday nights.

We've also had a least one son in public school since 1996 until Jason graduates in 2019. When Jason had his high school orientation, I was amazed when the teacher who taught Billy ninth grade Algebra recognized me from a decade earlier when Billy was there. When Jason and I walked outside of a building, the teacher did a double take at us, and said, "Hey, I know you guys." Of course, the fact that Jason looks a lot like Billy helped him to identify me—but probably confused him, too, as if he were stepping back in time. Then an English teacher of David's recognized me too. It was a rather odd sense of déjà vu.

Throughout the years, the boys were of course at different places along the road to maturity, so the body changes were sometimes a source of insight for them and for me. Once when Billy was 15, he was lying on the couch asleep, his arm stretched out over his head. Jason, 6, surveyed his brother's exposed underarm hair and screwed up his face in disgust. I grinned and explained, "That's what happens when you get older."

He pursed his lips for a second and then showed disgust again. "The thought of that happening to me *sickens* me," he said.

There was however, one big advantage of this large age gap between sons: the older boys provided very convenient built-in babysitters for Jason when he was growing up. And that, sometimes, outweighs all the disadvantages.

The Caboose Baby

Starting over with the baby routine after your other children are in school has its ups and downs. Sure there were times at the mall I had to yell to David, who was six when Jason was a baby, "Don't do wheelies with the stroller!" And yes, it was a pain to have to take the diaper bag with me again wherever we went, after going places hands-free for several years.

The age gap means that I was considered an older mom when I had Jason. A mid-life mom, as they also call it, since I had him when I was 38. I've heard kids who were born awhile after their siblings is often called a caboose baby. The last one, bringing up the rear, giving the illusion of straggling behind. This analogy is a sad one to me, as if the caboose is an afterthought, trying to keep up with the rest of the train. Jason was no afterthought; he was what I knew was needed to complete our family, and though he sometimes tries my patience, he has been a delight to have for a son. I much prefer the moniker 'bonus baby', another name I've heard for the children born considerably later than their siblings.

I, too, was a caboose baby or bonus baby, since my brother is 13 years older than I am, and my sisters are 11 and 8 years older. My mother was also 38 when she had me, but I was the only child actually planned, or at least that's what she tells me. "I knew I wanted another baby," my mother told me, and so they decided to have one more. I was born on Mother's Day, which I have to say was incredibly good timing on my part. But I was the youngest, the 'baby' of the family, and perhaps that's why I wanted a caboose baby too. One to hold, to savor, knowing it's your last. And knowing from personal experience that yes, time really does go by quickly and he'll be grown in no time.

Years ago I knew a woman who had four children within six years because she said they wanted to "get the baby stuff over with and be done with it." I understand her rationale, but I cherished the baby years and didn't mind going through them again, even though it meant starting over with a third one much younger than his siblings. Starting over was exciting because we got to revisit those baby years—and we'd be enjoying it with our older boys.

I remember what it was like to be the caboose, to try to do what the older siblings do, which for me was playing the "Mystery Date" board game and writing stories about boyfriends since I was too little to have one myself like they did. Though we remained close emotionally, I watched my siblings grow too old for me to really do things with—too old for us to have many activities in common. My sisters used to play tennis, and my job, which I took great pride in, was to retrieve the tennis balls when they went over the fence (evidently my sisters weren't very good because I remember chasing a lot of balls). And I recall very well the years when my sisters were dating and I was at the age where all their beaus were like mysterious movie stars to me. My sisters would wait impatiently for their boyfriends to call them and in the meantime, they'd write the boys' names in big block letters on the side of the telephone directory. I actually can recall their former boyfriends' names better now than they can because the whole dating scene had such a big impact on me.

Jason always liked to do things with his brothers, but as Billy and David got older, the age gap became more pronounced. I realized this when my two oldest boys first wanted to go to the State Fair with friends instead of family, leaving me to take Jason by myself, which I knew was less fun for him. So I called a good friend of his and took him to the fair with us so Jason would have someone to ride the roller coaster and the Flying Bobs with. My mother and I used to go to the fair with my best friend, Tina, and her mom, who conveniently happened to be my mother's best friend. The four of us would have a terrific time together, and I still treasure those memories. Jason's friend, however, had two younger siblings at home, and so his mom had to stay with them. These are the logistics of being an older mom when it seems all the other moms are younger with toddlers still running around.

Then on Halloween night of 2008, I became completely depressed as Jason and I wandered the dark streets of our neighborhood practically alone. When I'd gone trick or treating with Billy and David, there had been other kids their age and other moms my age going trick or treating too. The streets had been packed, and the neighborhood kids shouted and cavorted, as they dashed up and down hills with their little plastic pumpkin flashlights and candy buckets held tight in their hands. But everybody in our neighborhood was now evidently too old for Halloween; there were very few moms and kids to be seen and many houses remained dark. Jason was dressed as a really cool Indiana Jones, and I felt bad that nobody was around to see his costume. I longed for the Halloween nights when our streets had been ablaze with lights and excitement. Was I the only mom out there anymore?

Our family vacations have changed too as Billy and David have schedule conflicts with jobs, internships, and courses that don't fit into vacation plans easily any more. This means that my husband Kevin, Jason, and I will be taking more vacations with just the three of us. I did the same thing with my parents when my siblings eventually stopped going on family vacations. I welcome the time to concentrate on just Jason, but I know I'll also miss the times we were all together at Disney or at a Red Sox game or even in our old camper. I'll miss having my boys together, and I know, as one caboose baby to another, that Jason will miss it too.

Kevin and I took Jason to San Diego and LA during spring break of his freshman year of high school, and it was fun, and the weather was great. However, we all felt something missing; it was odd to be a family of three. Yet, we did make some good memories with just Jason, so I hope that was special for him, as I know it was for Kevin and me.

I realize also that I'm not the same mom with Jason as I was with David and Billy. When Jason was younger, I'd try to go out and shoot hoops with Jason like I did them, but sometimes the back and the knees weren't very willing. The hardest part is when Jason himself realized I wasn't young anymore. One night when he was four, we were about to say our bedtime prayers, when Jason asked me, "Are you going to get old, Mom?" I didn't know where this question came from, if there had been anything that had happened that day or anything anybody had said to him that prompted this. I decided to tread gingerly on this topic. I explained to him that everybody gets older, that life would be boring if we stayed the same. He reached out to hug me, sobbing, "I don't want you to get old!" My heart ached right then because Billy and David had never said that to me before, and I wondered if this was a result of his being a caboose baby. I pulled him to me and kissed the top of his head, as his tears wet my shoulder. He said again through his sobs, "I don't want you to get old." He asked me if I was going to be as old as Grandma, and I told him I hoped so because that would mean that I'd live a long, healthy life. I then added that I wouldn't be as old as Grandma for a long time. I held him for a while longer there on his bed, rocking him slightly back and forth in my arms. My baby. My caboose baby.

When my older two boys were young, I knew other moms with sons the same age and formed relationships with them; with Jason, I didn't do that as much because the moms of his friends were younger and traveled in different circles than I did, while I was busy with my older sons. When Jason was in elementary school, I'd find myself longing for the days when the moms of my child's friends were my age, and we formed close friendships. So often Jason and I did things together by ourselves. Nothing wrong with that, but I find myself remembering how Billy and David used to play together and pal around on vacations. I didn't want Jason to be lonely or bored.

As a caboose baby myself, I can relate to this predicament. My mother was lucky enough to have some friends and relatives with children near my age, but the two of us frequently did things by ourselves together. When I was searching for a card for my mom on Mother's Day several years ago, I found the perfect one: on the cover, it read, "From Your Youngest". I immediately picked it out of the Hallmark card rack and read it, getting tears in my eyes. I had never seen such a card before that was from a youngest child; perhaps there is such a growing number of caboose babies now that a card like this was needed. It read in part: *"Baby of the family? I was, I guess, it's true. But I didn't mind the slightest bit because, Mom, I had you."* When I gave it to my mother, I told her I would read it to her, which I do quite often since her eyesight is poor due to macular degeneration. But this time as I read, I got a lump in my throat, looking into her blue eyes and also knowing Jason was right there listening too. I wrote inside the card, "I hope I can be the mom to Jason that you were to me when my siblings were grown up." My mother and Jason will never know how very much I meant that. I had my mom, and now my youngest child had me. And I, in turn, still had him. It seems like some sort of circle of life, and I relish the fact that I am an older mom. I vow to savor the time I still have with him at home, as it dwindles day by day.

That Independent Streak

The independent streak is extremely strong in caboose babies, so older moms have to adapt to it. Caboose babies will be more daring than their older siblings were. A case in point is swimming lessons. When my oldest, Billy, was seven, he decided to take the biggest granddaddy swim test of them all at the YMCA—the black band test. If a swimmer could swim to the other side of the pool and dogpaddle for three minutes, then he would earn a coveted 'black band', which gave them the privilege of jumping off the diving board into the nine-foot water without parental supervision. He was nervous about his taking the test, and so was I. Billy had practiced for it and planned exactly when he was going to take it. I watched him swim the length of the pool, my own heart pounding.

It was a big deal when he passed the test and was awarded the band. I think we all went out to eat that night. When the guys were younger and they'd achieved something on a particular day, I made it a point to tell Kevin about the achievement such as a great score on a test—or in this case, the black band—followed by the fact that the son who had achieved it wanted to know if we could go out to eat that night to celebrate. In fact, the son had never asked that—it was completely my idea, a genius plan in getting to eat at a restaurant without any resistance from Kevin. I miss those days. When the boys got older and I'd try to pull this, they'd reply, "I didn't say I wanted to go to eat, Mom." Which would make me look really bad, like I was milking my child's achievement for personal gain. Which I was.

But my experience with Billy's black band achievement was much different from what happened with Jason's swim test. With Jason, I didn't even know he was planning to take the test. He decided without any fanfare at all to arrange with a lifeguard to take the test himself. The test was given in the lifeguards' ten minute break time when everyone was out of the pool. Jason had just finished swim lessons, and I'd thought he was headed over to the splash area where kids could play among all sizes of water fountains.

So I was lying back on my lounge chair when I saw Jason and another kid standing on the poolside as if they were ready to jump in. "Jason!" I yelled out to him. "It's break time—you can't get in now." Then one of the lifeguards came up beside him and blew a whistle, at which point, Jason jumped in and began to swim across the pool with the lifeguard looking on. That's when I realized Jason was taking the big swim test. He'd been so cavalier about it that he'd evidently decided to take it on a whim. I watched him glide across the pool, a faint smile on my lips as I admired his independence. Jason passed the test and received his black band just like his brothers. I will always remember the look of pride on his face as he walked over to me afterwards. A caboose baby milestone.

Another time this streak showed up in Jason was when I took him to a theme park to ride a new roller coaster. He had just turned ten and went with an eleven-year-old friend who was also a roller coaster lover. I am not a lover of roller coasters, so my plan was to let them ride the rides while I sat and read a book. But this roller coaster was incredibly steep, and Jason's friend was hesitant to get on it. Undeterred, Jason said, "Okay, I'll ride it first and check it out." It was autumn, so the lines weren't long, so pretty soon there he was at the front of the line. My other boys never did this, and I felt a twinge of motherly guilt letting him get on the ride by himself. Yet, he wasn't scared at all. Independent streak? Perhaps it was more like a daredevil streak.

I lost track of Jason once he got on the ride, but as I watched the coaster climb the tracks and then drop rapidly down the huge hill, I held my breath, saying a prayer my boy was doing okay up there. When the ride was over, Jason came running over, yelling to his friend, "It was awesome!" That was all the encouragement the friend needed, so he joined Jason as they raced back to the line to get on the ride. They both liked it so much that they rode it several times in a row.

And Jason was no caboose. He sat right up in the front, ready for adventure.

Little Brotheritis

Jason has long suffered from a severe case of Little Brotheritis. This is when Jason thinks he can do anything his brothers do just the way they do it even though they are considerably older. When he was seven, he played in a local basketball rec league, in which they did not allow double teaming. The trouble was most of the kids didn't understand what double-teaming was, so they did it anyway. Jason, having watched many of his brothers' games knew precisely what double teaming was, and so it irritated him when the other team was doing it to him.

A few times in one particular game, I heard Jason shout, "No double teaming!" but to no avail. The referees in the league were high school kids who seemed afraid to blow their whistles. I could see the frustration building in Jason, and it was getting a little rough on both sides with fouls not being called. Finally, with about three minutes to play, Jason dribbled in for a lay-up and was about to shoot when suddenly there were two boys—one of them much taller—guarding Jason with their hands up in the air, making it impossible for Jason to shoot or even move. "No double teaming!" he yelled again, but both kids stayed put. So Jason, no doubt remembering the aggressive games he saw his brothers play in high school, elbowed the tall guy right in the gut. The guy bent over, clutching his stomach, and the parents watching in the stands all said "Owww" in unison. The ref blew his whistle, and the coaches decided to take Jason out of the game. Officially, I'd guess you'd say, he'd been ejected. Probably the first ever ejection of a kid in the Mighty Mites league, and it had happened to my son. Kevin and I felt terrible. Jason had to sit on the bench with the team even though he couldn't play.

The boy who got hit recovered quickly and even continued to play the last few minutes of the game, but Kevin and I felt like everyone was looking at Jason and envisioning what his face would someday look like on a "Wanted" poster. The thing was the incident had occurred right under the basket near where the parents sat, so we all had a good view of things as they unfolded and had seen the scowl on Jason's face and his determination when he drew back his elbow. It was definitely intentional. When the game was finally over, we had him apologize to the boy, who seemed to be okay. We held Jason out of the next game and wrote a note of apology to the coach.

Kevin says he will always remember going home that day and telling Billy and David what had happened. "Your brother got ejected from the game," he told them, as their disbelief turned to uncontrollable laughter. Sibling support at its finest. Their laughter infuriated an already upset Jason, but they couldn't contain it.

Littlebrotheritis, I fear, is not just something that happens when they are young but rather something that continues through the years. A chronic illness that just manifests itself in different ways as they get older. 'Cause he will always be the little brother.

Hand-Me-Downs

With the addition of a third child in our house, we became very familiar with the hellacious world of hand-me-downs and how they seem to take over a household when you pass clothes and toys from one child to another and then to another. Sure it saves money, but they were EVERYWHERE, filling closets and every nook & cranny in our home. Ideally, we'd love to have a walk-up attic or some other storage area, but we've never had that. I wish I had it then for hand-me-downs and now for all the stuff the boys leave behind in their bedrooms when they move out, as well as for boxes of memorabilia from throughout the years.

Back in the days right before Jason was born, I had to undertake the task of rearranging our household in preparation for the new baby—a challenge made even tougher since we were also adding onto the family room of our house. One part of that task was to pull out all of the hand-me-downs from storage and organize them by size for the baby. Kevin came home after work one day to find me sitting in the middle of David's room, surrounded by piles of clothes, cardboard boxes, and toys. I was leaning back against one of the stacks of clothes, a dazed expression on my face, overwhelmed with my closet-cleaning project.

I looked at Kevin and sighed. "Don't ya just hate it when you lose your motivation for a project right in the middle of it?" I asked.

"What's this?" he said, pointing at a stack of toys.

"Things that need batteries."

"Wonderful," he replied sarcastically, knowing full well if they required Double A's we only have Triple-A, and if they needed C-cell, we'd only have D.

"We need more storage space," I commented.

"Why don't you throw out some of the junk from the cabinet in the family room?"

"You're talking about my old albums and 45-speed records again, aren't you," I asked him, perturbed.

"Sharon, there's a "Meet the Brady Bunch' album back there."

"And sure to one day be a collector's item," I retorted. I admit I'm a bit of a pack rat, especially when it comes to sentimental things. It's especially hard for me to part with all those drawings and art projects the boys do at school. And with a third child, we'd need even more space.

Hand-me-downs are great in theory: all the outgrown clothes are passed down to younger brothers or sisters, thus saving money in the long run. One of the most frequent comments I heard when people found out I was expecting a third boy was, "Well, at least you already have the clothes." In practice, however, hand-me-downs aren't quite the wonderful thing they're made out to be, particularly when there is a nine year gap between your kids, and you have to find a place to store those hand-me-downs during all that time. I realized this that day as I sat surrounded by about twenty-five boxes of Billy and David's old clothes—everything from infant to size 6—trying to organize all of it for the arrival of Boy #3 in just a few weeks.

Once I got David's room organized, I took on the nursery. What really made it frustrating was the lack of size tags on the clothes so it was difficult to tell if something was 12 months size or 18 months. It was a tedious task. Kevin called up to me about thirty minutes after I started sorting and said in all seriousness, "Ya done yet?" Men can't comprehend what an undertaking sorting clothes is.

I've always been amused by how pregnant women are said to be 'nesting' when they start cleaning up to prepare for their baby as their delivery date draws near. To me, this isn't any kind of innate motherly instinct but simply the fact that the mother-to-be knows that soon family and friends will be swarming into her house to see the newborn, and she'd better clean up while she has a chance.

So I was feeling some pressure to get all of this done before I gave birth. We were also under pressure to get the renovations done to our house. The plan was to divide our two-room open living area with a wall, separating it into a study and family room. We needed the study so we'd have a place to put our computers, books, and files; all that had been in the large bonus room which had been a combination study and playroom. However, with the addition of another baby to the family, the bonus room would become Billy's room, Billy's room would become David's room, and David's small room would become the baby's nursery. Got all that? We knocked down the back walls of the family room and kitchen eating area to extend the rooms for a more spacious look with windows looking onto a greenway. Good plan in theory. But due to numerous construction delays, the plan took a lot longer than we first had thought. How long? Put it this way, we had a port-a-potty in our yard for construction worker use for seven months, from October until April, and the only work that got done was knocking down the old front porch.

Actually, during those seven months, we grew rather attached to our port-a-potty. At Christmas, Kevin strung it with colored lights. Needless to say, no one in the neighborhood had decorations quite like it. And it was very easy to give directions to our house: "Go about a half mile and we're on the left. There's a port-a-potty in the front yard. You can't miss it."

When the rare big snowstorm of 2000 hit, covering North Carolina with over two feet of snow, the downhill driveway provided a great sledding place. There was that one time, though, that six-year-old David lost control of his sled and slammed into the plastic port-a-potty, his body hitting the side of it with arms outstretched and then sliding down the side of it like a cartoon character. I'm surprised we didn't have a cut-out of David's body left in the port-a-potty wall like Wiley Coyote used to have after his battles with the Road Runner. But being a boy, he got up a little dazed and said, "That was fun!" (Actually, David didn't really lose control of the sled; he scared me because I saw he was going so fast, so I put my foot on the sled as it went by to slow him down. But I forgot some property of physics that caused the sled to slow down but caused David to fly off the sled into the port-a-potty. I have apologized for this many times.)

We began to think we'd never be rid of our port-a-potty and entertained the idea of tying an "It's a boy" sign and a blue bow to it once the baby was born. But in late April the day finally did come that the port-a-potty put there by our first contractor was taken away at last. As we watched them tow it up the hill, I felt a little emotional; it had been in our yard so long, it felt like it belonged there. A few neighbors gathered in the yard to watch as they carted it off on the truck. Weirdly, I had to resist the urge to wave good-bye.

Then the work on the house finally got underway. By the time Jason was born, the house was almost complete, but the hardwood floors still had to be installed. So we slept over at my parents' house for a few nights after he was born so the work could be finished. Finally, the work was all done, and we—all five of us—went home to our newly renovated downstairs. Unfortunately, the upstairs was still a mess, covered with hand-me-downs and boxes.

Kevin and I have sometimes looked at the exquisite homes for sale on the Parade of Homes tour. We certainly weren't looking to buy, but we still liked to look. When we returned home from one of these tours, Kevin remarked, "The biggest difference between our house and those houses on the tour was they didn't have clothes lying all around." Thinking of the spiral staircases, the double ovens, the plush theatre rooms, and the basement game rooms that those Parade houses had, I said, "Well, I don't think it's the *biggest* difference." I've resigned myself to the fact that our house will always have clothes lying around with a couple of baskets of unfolded laundry by the steps. And of course, hand-me-downs taking up closet space. Hand-me-downs aren't just clothes either, but toys and sports equipment. I'll never forget the day that Jason started roller hockey lessons, and not wanting to buy another expensive pair of roller blades, we had Jason wear an old pair of David's. After that first lesson, the instructor motioned me over and said, "Those skates your son is wearing are really worn down. I'm afraid he'll turn his ankle in them or something." Oops.

From Billy to David to Jason. At one point, I thought hand-me-downs would never end. But their days are coming to an end. At the age of 15, Jason suddenly caught up to David's height of 6 feet 2 and even shot past that, meaning that David would no longer be passing anything down to him. Billy, at 6 feet 6 will still occasionally pass tee shirts or Polo sweaters down to his brothers, so there are still a few boxes of things upstairs. I kept some of the boys' baby clothes in a chest in our bedroom, and I come across them every now and then. I finger the soft material and imagine their little bodies filling up the outfit as I used to hold them against me as they slept. Those tiny onesie sleepers take me right back to those times in their lives. So they will stay in the cedar chest in the bedroom; I'm not handing those down to anyone—except maybe a grandchild in the future.

The Art of Brown Nosing

Being the older mother of a caboose kid, I had to remember that Jason learned from his brothers and thus, became older acting very quickly. He had a quick wit and terrific vocabulary at an early age, which made him seem more mature than a lot of his peers. As the youngest, Jason figured out a few things, which kept me on my toes. I never knew what Jason would say, particularly when he talked to adults. He loved to have conversations with grown-ups and was quite honest and frank about his feelings, even political opinions or—God help us—things that might go on in our household.

There have been many times when I was engaged in a conversation with someone at an event when I realized that Jason and an adult were in deep conversation with Jason doing most of the talking. Definitely a red flag. I would immediately start sweating bullets, wondering and worrying what on earth he was talking about with them. I'd lose total concentration on the conversation I was having as I tried to overhear what Jason was saying. Usually it was all okay, and the adult would later tell me what a charming boy Jason was. Jason understood the art of brown nosing, that way some people have of giving compliments when the ulterior motive is winning favor with someone. Also known as sucking up and a few other choice phrases. Examples: When Jason was 7, we took Grandma O'Donnell out to eat for her birthday. On the way home, she thanked us, and Jason responded, "It was our pleasure, Grandma." Grandma O'Donnell beamed.

"Oh, isn't that nice," she said. Billy sitting in the back behind Jason clenched his teeth together and punched his fist into his hand, as if saying, "Why I oughta ..."

When Jason went to spend the night with his friend Watson, Watson's mom was getting ready to read a book to her two-year-old daughter. Jason said to the mom, "I'd be happy to read that to her." And he did, and the little girl loved it. Watson's mom sent me an email afterwards to let me know how sweet she thought it was. Billy and David rolled their eyes in exasperation when they heard it and said in unison, "Suck-up."

When Jason started attending a private school for one school year, he evidently wanted to make sure he made a good impression. The name of the school was Thales Academy, a new school in the area. One of the assignments was to write about what you would do if you were President. Jason wrote he would find a cure for cancer and build more Thales Academies. I do think Jason was sincere in writing this, but he also knew it never hurts to score brownie points with the teacher or administrators who just might see his paper hanging on the wall.

The boy does know how to position himself for the maximum desired effect. I realized this when he was seven and he and I were watching one of those tear jerking episodes of "Extreme Home Makeover." It was a heart-wrenching one about a military serviceman injured in Iraq who had several kids and then his wife left him. It showed people crying as they talked about all that the man had gone through. "Boy," said Jason, "this show has a lot of emotion." At the end of the show after the beautiful new house had been unveiled, the announcer gave the address to write to if you wanted to nominate a family for the show. Jason's eyes grew wide. "Hey, Mom, can we be one of the families on the show?"

I explained to him that the families on that show had all been through very sad things in their lives that had made it difficult to afford a home. I added, "Those families usually have someone sick or injured or something really sad like that."

"It's sad that Granddaddy O'Donnell died," Jason said.

"Yes, it was," I agreed, "but that was a long time ago and it didn't affect whether or not we had a house to live in. That show chooses families who've been affected by some kind of tragedy."

Jason raised his eyebrows and held out his right arm, palm facing up, like he was one of the girls on The Price is Right revealing the showcase of the day. He said, "Little Jason O'Donnell ... never got to meet his grandfather." I think I'm raising a future public relations executive or perhaps, and I shudder to think it, a politician.

A Real Christmas Tree

When Jason was ten, he and I were driving past a Christmas tree lot several weeks before Christmas, and I saw in the rear-view mirror that he was looking at the trees longingly. I thought of the nice fake tree that we've had the past four years—the one that requires no water, the one that retains the same shape year after year (wish I could say that for myself) and doesn't require cutting off limbs to make it fit in the tree stand, the one that doesn't drop its needles behind requiring constant vacuuming. Such convenience. So I turned the radio up, hoping the moment would pass. Then came the words. "I wish we could have a real tree this year," Jason sighed.

"But the tree we have now fits the spot by the window in the family room perfectly," I responded, smiling at him to hide the guilt I felt by denying him the same memories I'd had at the holidays and even the ones my older sons—ages 19 and 16—had. I felt bad because I knew that Jason was paying the price for being the third child and so much younger than his brothers. Mom and Dad had simply gotten tired of the whole live tree scenario by the time Jason was a pre-schooler. "Besides," I added, "you've had a real tree before."

"Yeah, but I can barely remember it." I quickly did the math in my head and realized that he was probably right. When our family finally succumbed to the logic of buying an artificial tree, Jason had been only six years old.

His memory of the years we had a real tree might indeed be foggy. "I can sort of remember going to pick out the tree, and that was really fun," Jason said staring dreamily out the window at yet another Christmas tree lot. They were everywhere, it seemed. I wanted to cave—to say okay, we'd go pick out a real tree. But that fake one was already standing in the family room just waiting for decorations. It'd be so much easier, so much less time-consuming, just to go with the fake one again this year.

But Jason was 10. And next year he'd be 11, and then the teenage years wouldn't be far behind. I, of all people, should know how quickly a boy goes from being a bright-eyed child filled with wonder to a skeptical teen on the brink of manhood. But that damn tree stand, what a pain it was to get the trunk of the tree to fit just right and then to have hold the tree up in place while my husband got under the tree and turned the screws on the stand to tighten it—only to discover the thing was leaning to the left instead of being straight, so we'd have to repeat the process all over.

Ah, but the aroma of real trees. There is nothing like it that signifies Christmas is here. When a real tree is in the house, you know it as soon as you come inside. I can remember standing by the tree when I was a little girl and leaning over close to the branches, taking a deep breath, savoring the aroma of evergreen or fir. As I stopped the car at a red light, I turned and looked at my son and asked, "Do you really want a real tree?" Wide-eyed, he nodded his head up and down quickly. Then sensing he might be about to get what he wanted, he smiled. Not willing to agree totally to such a sanity-altering decision, I told him, "Let me talk to Dad about it." Yes, Jason now had hope, but he also knew that his Dad is a frugal person who can calculate in his head how much we've saved over the years by having an artificial tree. There was still some convincing to do.

Help arrived in the form of a letter from Jason's school that he pulled from his backpack when we got home. It was a congratulatory letter because Jason had qualified for the Duke University Talent Identification Program since he scored in the 99% in reading on a recent national test. When Kevin walked in the door that night, Jason and I shared the good news with him. He told Jason how proud he was of him and had Jason call his grandmother to tell her. Then I knew it was the right time to bring up the Christmas tree request. "Jason," I said, "tell Dad what you want this Christmas." And he did, with the awe and excitement of a 10-year-old.

We went to pick out a real tree that afternoon.

Speed Version of the Birds and the Bees Talk

When Jason was 11, I decided to finally have 'the talk' about the facts of life with him. With my two older sons, I had the talk when they were ten; but, I kept putting off the talk with my youngest. I'd gone through some facts about puberty when he was younger because the questions would naturally evolve as he saw his older brothers grow. I'd also talked to him about the private areas issue when he was much younger, but the actual sex talk got put off somehow. I don't really know why other than perhaps I still think of him as my baby. But I knew that in the last part of the fifth grade (which was rapidly approaching) the teachers would send home that note I'd gotten twice before—the one saying the last science unit the class would study would be human growth (puberty) and reproduction. That was my deadline. I knew I didn't want my son to be the only kid in class to be blindsided by some really startling information. Yep, it was time for the talk. Of course, I'd answered a few curious questions from him over the years, but I hadn't delved into the topic the way I needed to do yet.

With Billy and David, I prepared notes to make sure I gave them all the information both factually and about the way I feel about sex and relationships from a moral point of view. I chose a time at home to talk with each one alone, and then I did so. Both of them seemed to be ignoring me as I spoke, but I knew they were taking in all the information. Then afterwards, I left some very good sexual education books with them for them to read and told them to ask me any questions if they needed to do so. I began to prepare the same for my youngest and got out the educational books and put them on my bedroom dresser near the door. I was going to sit down and jot down some notes beforehand like I did with my other boys, but alas, that was not to be. Instead, I ended up giving an impromptu talk.

So when I picked up my youngest from school one day, he handed me the note—the one from the teachers letting parents know the birds and the bees topic would be covered in school in a few days and requesting permission from parents. I sighed as I read the note. I needed to talk to my son that night—couldn't put it off any longer. But he had a baseball game that night and so did my middle son, and there were some other things going on too. And there we were in the car right then— alone—and I wouldn't have to worry about making eye contact as much because I'd be driving. I knew that boys wouldn't feel as awkward if there was less eye contact involved. I decided to go ahead and do the talk right there in the car while my son was basically a captive audience.

I launched into the talk and found that it was pretty easy. Perhaps too easy. My car version of this information was done at a much quicker pace than when I had talked to my older boys at home. I was on a roll and feeling relieved that I was finally getting 'the talk' checked off my list of things to do. But somewhere between explaining how the uterus prepares for a baby and sperm production, I glanced over at my son. His eyes were wide, but his brow was furrowed, and his expression was one of disbelief and disgust. He looked over at me like as if to say 'what the hell are you talking about?" I laughed and realized I needed to slow down. I got the job done, despite a few "Okay, mom" comments that I think were intended to make me stop. Bless his heart. When I was done, he mumbled, "TMI", which I knew stood for 'too much information.'

But hey, the talk was all over by the time we'd pulled into the driveway, including the part about how anybody can have sex, that it doesn't make you grown up or truly popular, and that ideally sex is meant for marriage or a committed relationship between adults and that it should not be something taken casually. I knew while saying this that the media he sees around him often does take sex and promiscuity casually. It's so tough to express values to our children when so much around them shows them things that are contradictory. Whenever I hear people say that such values are antiquated or that my views are from another generation, it really gets to me. I've told my sons and nephews and nieces before that the passage of time does not mean that a person's morals should change—that doesn't equate to 'progress' at all. Each generation thinks it is somehow more insightful or cooler than the last generations, but basically, people are the same. They still have the same feelings, the same need for relationships. They suffer the same kind of broken hearts and revel in the same kind of falling head-over-in-heels-in-love. And with all of that goes the importance of having respect for yourself and others—no matter what decade it happens to be. I felt this same way in college in the early '80s when my generation was the cool one.

My views on this topic sometimes make me feel more antiquated than being an older mom does. They are views that I believe in, and I want to make sure my sons understand why, so this is always part of 'the talk.'

And let me also apologize to my youngest son for giving him the facts of life talk in the car. Didn't realize how fast I was talking while driving. Too much information conveyed in too much of a matter-of-fact tone. I can only attribute that to his being the youngest of three, and sometimes I suffer burn-out and just want to check things off my list. No excuse, though. Sorry, son. But to his credit, he actually brought home the puberty hand-out from school and shared it with me, even telling me some of the vocabulary words they'd discussed. My older sons would never have done that. I guess the Birds and the Bees Speed Version wasn't so ineffective after all.

But evidently, I went into more detail than I had to in order to prepare him for the class. When I asked what they had talked about specifically, he said that they hadn't gotten into a lot of the things I'd talked about with him. He added, "You know, we just talked about scrotums and stuff." I didn't know it'd be that simple. Scrotums and stuff. Sounds like a catchy name for one of those eclectic boutique shops somewhere. And it certainly epitomizes my house.

III
How I Got My Wrinkles

"We (older moms) have more life experience, thus more wisdom to share."

—Robin Gorman Newman,
founder of Motherhood Later ...Than Sooner
www.motherhoodlater.com

School Days, School Days

"Whew! They're out the door!" That's what I would think each weekday morning as Billy and David would finally leave the house when they were in elementary school. No matter how early we got up, mornings were always rushed with shouts of "Where are my shoes, Mom?" The morning time chore I dreaded the most when the guys were younger was making lunches. Stocking up at the grocery store on things like peanut butter, jelly, turkey, canned fruit, grapes, pretzels, and cookies. It was a constant shopping list I kept in my head, knowing the pantry had to stay full from week-to-week. I was lucky during Billy's first two school years when he wanted to buy his lunch instead of taking it from home. Then came that fateful day when he spotted the Godzilla lunchbox on a shelf at a local store, and my life was never the same.

Even when they got older, Billy and David still preferred to take their lunches from home rather than stand in long lunch lines. They made them sometimes, but usually it was easier for me or Kevin to do it, and we'd also have a little bit of control over what kind of nutrition goes into it. When Jason started kindergarten, Kevin and I accepted the fact that we'd have to start making three lunches instead of two; but, Jason decided that he wanted to buy his lunch at school. After he first told me this, I knelt beside him, tears welling in my eyes as I put my hand on his shoulder. "Bless you my son," I told him. After having gone through the elementary and middle school years with the other boys, I quite frankly, was not in the mood to have to start the lunch-making process over with boy number 3.

It was the actual making of the lunches that really gets to me—the monotony of it, the assembly line procedure, the routine, particularly when Billy and David were in elementary school. As I would spread peanut butter on sandwiches and put pineapple tidbits in little plastic cups, my mind wandered and I sometimes found myself thinking of Alice, the happy-go-lucky maid on The Brady Bunch. Remember how she fixed all those lunches—six of them in brown paper bags—and stood at the end of the stairs each morning as the kids came down, handing each of them their lunch, while she smiled the whole time, wishing Greg, Marcia, and the rest of them a great day?

As I made those lunches, I'd think about that, and felt bad that I complained about making two when she happily made six. How did Alice do it? One of those mornings, I mentioned this to my family, and Billy looked at me incredulously, like he thought I was about to snap and said to me slowly, "Mom—it was a TV show." Still, my hat is off to Alice.

David was especially difficult to get moving in the morning, always has been. When he was younger, several times we literally had to pull him out of his bed by his feet and flop him on the floor, but he still didn't wake up. Before cell phones were around, we set multiple alarm clocks by his bed, and he slept right through all the bells, whistles, radio music, and even a contraption that shook his bed to wake him up. We finally got one of those little glass timers with sand in it and told him if he got downstairs all dressed and ready to go before the sand ran out, then he would get a prize. That worked for about a week. We became very proficient at getting David to school just in the nick of time by taking short cuts, speeding, and going through yellow lights. I felt kind of like a racecar driver on the NASCAR circuit. Even in high school, David was tough to get moving in the mornings, even with the help of cell phone alarms; sometimes after he took a shower, he'd wrap a towel around him and go back to his room where we'd find him lying on his bed again. He claimed this was the way he dried his back. Drying your back by lying down on a bed with your eyes closed? Uh-huh, that sounds legit. During Billy's senior year, he took freshman brother David with him. Now that sounds like the perfect plan, but Billy is always punctual, while David takes twenty minutes to get out of the bed after awakened and then gets even slower. Billy would sit in the car in the driveway and blow the horn, which David would totally ignore. Our next door neighbor told me one day, "I see Billy out there waiting for David in the mornings, and I can just see the steam coming off his head." I'm not sure, but I think this is the way Cain and Able started out.

Now that it's just Jason at home, he has adopted David's slow-as-a-snail morning pace. Even slower if possible. At least we can call him on his cell phone to wake him up, but sometimes it goes right to voicemail. Two phone calls and no answer means that Kevin will take our dog, Fenway, to Jason's room to bark at him and lick his face. Any attempt to tell Jason that he is running late is always met with the same, "I know." Well if he knows, then why doesn't he get moving?

And then there's breakfast to deal with. Hey, I think a bowl of cereal should be just fine. Maybe some oatmeal. Billy and David loved the instant oatmeal with brightly-colored dinosaurs in it; to be honest, I think they still eat it even though they are in their 20s. Sometimes I make bacon and eggs, but usually my guys don't like to eat that in the mornings and on weekends, we often do pancakes or French toast from scratch. But never on weekdays.

When all three were living at home, some mornings we were doing good if all three boys had time to grab a Pop Tart for breakfast on their way out the door. I really hate it when teachers gave them projects where they had to write down what they ate for a week. You can't tell me that half that stuff isn't made-up by parents too embarrassed to write down what they really did feed their kids.

In our ever-growing county, school reassignment has often wreaked havoc on families' schedules, and ours has been touched, too. Billy was reassigned in third grade, which was upsetting for him then but turned out okay, although he did lose touch with some friends over time. Then it happened again when a new high school opened before his sophomore year, and he was reassigned to the new school, which was at least twice the distance than it was from our house to his former school. It was also a drive through heavy traffic near research companies as thousands of people commuted to work. A car trip that should take you 15 minutes would take you 35 or more one way. Usually, Billy took the bus since the school was so far out of the way, unlike the two schools the other guys went to, which were conveniently locate. He'd wake up at 5:15 to get the bus, David got up at 6 for Kevin to drive him, and Jason got up at 8:00 to go to the convenient school down the road. By the time I dropped off Jason at 9, our mornings with the guys were almost four hours long, and I hadn't even put on my make-up or turned on the computer yet.

The bus Billy rode didn't always come at the same time each morning and was unreliable. So a few times I'd have to take him to school, which meant I'd have to wake up Jason and have him ride with us. To get to Billy's high school, we had to drive through back roads; although the traffic is heavy due to the proximity of a Research Triangle Park, Billy's high school was located in the middle of nowhere with no fast food places or gas stations along the way. On one particular morning during the first few weeks of school, Billy's bus was late, so I pulled kindergartner Jason out of his bed and put him in the van so we could drive Billy. We were about five minutes away and running late, when Jason yelled that he had to poop. It wasn't like I could pull into a Shell station and let him run in because nothing was nearby. Nothing. And I'd taken the portable potty chair out of the SUV the previous year. I was racing to try to get Billy to school on time, so I shouted to Jason the only advice I could think of at the moment: "Squeeze your butt cheeks together!" Every time Jason would protest, I'd shout again, "Squeeze your butt cheeks together!" as I drove like a mad woman through the stretches of two lane, winding roads. By the time we arrived at the school, Jason had fallen asleep, poor little guy. With squeezed butt cheeks.

When we got back home, he woke up and went immediately into the bathroom. Later that day when Billy got home he said, "Mom, I was sitting in class and I started thinking about you yelling at Jason for him to squeeze his butt cheeks together, and I almost laughed out loud." Yes, I live only to make my children smile. At the time, though, it was a very serious situation. Actually, "Squeeze your butt cheeks together" isn't bad advice if you think about. It always makes you look skinnier in jeans.

Another thing about school days was the challenge of homework. We resorted to paying math tutors to help Billy and David because I certainly couldn't explain the stuff to them when I didn't understand it myself. Kevin is great at math, but he doesn't explain it in, shall we say, laymen's terms. He gets way too technical, one time even trying to help first-grader Jason with his math homework by doing algebraic equations when there was a much simpler way to do it. Poor Jason was totally confused. Not to mention the teacher.

Having conversations with the math tutors was always tough for me. They explained to me what they covered in a tutoring session with one of my boys and assumed that I, as a college-educated adult, would understand what they were saying. So I would nod my head a few times and say things like "Sure, I'll look over his quadratic equations" while containing the urge to scream at them, "I have no idea what you are talking about! That's why he has a tutor!"

Except for the higher math, helping with homework was usually my job, not Kevin's. But there have been times, though, that I wasn't there to help. One such night I read over the homework instructions with Jason and Kevin before I left home. The assignment that night was to write a poem. I left hastily, ready to go have dinner with some friends. As I was driving away, I thought to myself, *"What did I just do? I left Kevin of all people in charge of helping with poetry!"* When I returned home, Jason met me at the door with the poem his Dad had helped him with. After the first two lines, I knew we had a problem. Jason read, "When I got my dog Fenway I was really happy. Before I got him I'd been feeling pretty crappy."

"Wait a second," I interrupted, turning to Kevin. "You used the word crappy in a first grader's homework?"

He shrugged his shoulders. "What? It rhymes."

"I know they rhyme," I told him, "but maybe you could have chosen some other words." Kevin stared at me blankly. Jason stared at me blankly. I was fighting a losing battle.

And the things I've found in the boys' school backpacks. Once when David was in sixth grade, I noticed that his backpack had the distinct odor of vinegar to it. Upon investigating, I discovered a plastic baggie of old grapes left over from a long ago lunch crammed down into the corner of one of the side pockets. I don't know how the boy could ignore that smell for much longer. He was practically on his way to starting his own business: the David O'Donnell Vineyards. The backpack wasn't salvageable so we had to go buy another one ASAP.

I always appreciate the programs for the parents that teachers coordinate throughout the year, but I have to say with Jason, I was usually on pins and needles about what he might say or do during the program. He never did anything bad really; he was just ... Jason. For instance, at an end-of-the-year first grade program, students had used Power Point to make brief stories with pictures they had drawn along with their recorded voice-overs explaining the pictures. Jason was next to last of the 24 kids in presenting their work. I sat through some creative fiction stories, detailed non-fiction about whales and snakes, and even, to my amazement, a demonstration of how to do three digit addition with regrouping. When Jason got up there, he introduced the title of his presentation: "Random Thoughts by Jason O'Donnell".

All the parents and the teacher laughed, while I felt like disappearing into the floor. The presentation continued with a picture of a Red Sox game he'd drawn, a picture of the beach, and a picture of a road trip, which was nothing but a picture of black asphalt. At times like that, I'm reminded of Albert Einstein's quote, "Imagination is more important than knowledge." Even though I was aware that Jason had a lot of knowledge in addition to his creative side, I was still glad someone like Einstein said something like that.

Due to some overcrowding issues, we put Jason in private school for the second semester of second grade. It was an extra expense, and we had to cut back on some things, but we thought switching schools was in his best interest. He adjusted nicely, although the discipline was stricter.

The biggest transition for me was getting his uniform of solid collared shirts and khaki dress pants ironed and ready for him each day. For someone who despises ironing, this was cruel and unusual punishment. It had been so easy when he could just throw on a pair of jeans and t-shirt. It was especially tough because Jason was big for his age and was at that awkward stage where regular pants were slightly too tight, but husky pants were too big. So I had to buy husky ones and pay to have them tailored. By the first week of school, I finally had five pairs of dress pants that fit him perfectly hanging in his closet ready to go; I was so proud of myself. This was a 'mom thing', wanting to make sure my son was prepared to follow the dress code and would look nice. That next week, I went to pick him up one afternoon in the carpool line and saw to my horror that Jason's pants had a huge rip in the knee. He got in the car and said, "Mom, I made a 105 on my spelling test!"

I said, "Holy crap, what did you do to your pants?" Perhaps not the most supportive thing I could have said, but it was from the heart.

Our kids' school days sometimes seem like they are going to last forever; yet, with two of my boys now college grads, I realize they don't. And as my boys someday look back on those times, my voice will linger in their minds with that bit of sage wisdom from a mom who's been around the block a few times—squeeze your butt cheeks together.

Put It on the Calendar ...
I Mean Phone

My middle son, David, 14 at the time, shouted up the stairs to me the date of his next basketball practice. "Put it on the calendar!" I yelled down to him. As in THE calendar—the huge one that hung in the kitchen by the phone, telling us where to go when. This big master calendar is where we, ideally, were supposed to write down all sports practices and games, appointments, project due dates, and work schedules. If somebody didn't write an event on the calendar, then that was too bad; we would miss it. It was the little bit of organization that my house had, and I stuck by it. Without it, our house of chaos would be even worse.

It used to hang by the phone because the idea was that if Kevin or one of the boys got a phone call about a meeting or doctor appointment, then all they'd have to do was turn and write it immediately on the calendar. Worked in theory, but not in practice. My guys were never good with phones and phone etiquette anyway. One of the boys—I forget who—once left a phone message on a Band-Aid wrapper that was lying on the counter. I happened to notice it when I was about to throw the wrapper in the trash. And if someone called for me, but I was in the shower or maybe drying my hair, instead of putting the phone down and coming to find me, they'd bring the phone to the bathroom door, and yell, "Someone's on the phone for you!" The person on the other end of the line would hear everything and would know they were calling at an inconvenient time. You'd think this kind of common sense manners would go without saying. Not in our house when our boys were in elementary school.

There was one time long ago when we didn't need to rely on our calendar to guide our lives, a time when I used to never forget any event a family member was supposed to attend. But after Jason was born, part of my memory somehow disappeared, and I found myself forgetting to take the two older boys to games and birthday parties. One time we arrived at a party to discover it was the right place, right time, but the wrong day. When we went in, there sat a bunch of little girls we didn't know staring at us like we were aliens. So I bought the calendar back in 2000. At the suggestion of another mom, I even began to coordinate it by writing my sons' appointments and activities in different colors: my oldest son Billy's appointments in blue, David's in red, and Jason's in green. It took a little practice to get used to this method, but it definitely helped to remember things. However, eventually one of the colored markers would run out of ink or got misplaced, in which case, I'd grab another marker and write in the wrong color for that son, thus making a total mess of the calendar and defeating the whole purpose of the color coordination in the first place.

All of my family members used to rely on that master calendar, and over the years it became MY job to keep in updated. Like I had nothing else to do. I also wrote down certain errands or household chores for a particular day so I could stay focused. Every time I did this, though, I was reminded of an episode of a Berenstain Bear show in which the two little cubs and Papa Bear had to take over Mama Bear's household duties for a week. As they would mark each chore off the list, they'd smile at each other like they'd really accomplished something. "They're in for a rude awakening," I thought to myself. I'd like to see the expressions on their faces when they realized that mothers never get to 'mark off' a chore because we have to do it all over again within 48 hours. Mama Bear would have to do all those chores again as soon as she came home. But at least poor ole Mama Bear was able to get away for a few days. That's a tough thing for moms to do, and when we do manage it, we have to spend hours working on detailed lists and instructions to leave behind with our husbands.

Still, getting places on time is sometimes half the battle. When the boys were little, it was definitely a challenge. If it was a doctor or dentist appointment, we got there on time usually, but for other things, sometimes I felt we had a little more leeway. Yes, usually we were the ones sneaking into church during the first hymn or in the middle of a prayer, getting to a sports event after the kick-off or first pitch, or showing up a little late for family get-togethers. "We're always running late," 9-year-old Jason said to me one day as we pulled up a birthday party ten minutes behind schedule.

"No, we're not," I replied.

Billy, who was in the seat beside me, raised his eyebrows and looked at me bug-eyed like I'd just said the earth wasn't round. "Mom," he said, "sometimes when I have a dentist appointment we're cutting it so close you drop me off right at the front door, push me out of the car and yell, 'Run, run, run!'"

"But are you late?"

"Almost."

"But are you late?" I repeated, feeling like Perry Mason trying to make a point in court.

Billy finally relented, but I knew he had a very valid point. I'm just one of those people who tries to fill every moment; if we're running fifteen minutes early for something, I think, "Mmmm—what errand can we run in fifteen minutes so we don't waste the time?" Then we go by the dry cleaners or get milk at the store and end up frantically trying to make it to the original event in the nick of time. Usually, we do, but it's a stressful lifestyle. It's a bad sign when David once said after we arrived at a team event five minutes late, "Hey, this is the earliest we've ever been late."

When Jason was seven, we actually arrived at one of his indoor soccer games fifteen minutes early. He ran in ahead of me and then reappeared at the door, a perplexed expression on his face. "My team's not on the field," he exclaimed, somewhat alarmed. The poor little fellow was so used to running onto the field to join his teammates just as the starting whistle blew that he actually thought there was no game.

I smiled at him. "We're *early*," I said slowly, emphasizing the word since I knew it was a totally new concept to him. "The game doesn't start for another 15 minutes."

He stood there for a second, staring ahead, like the proverbial fish out of water. "What do I do?" he asked. Clearly, our family had some time management issues.

All these sporting events and appointments for everybody else often mean that appointments for 'mom' are at the bottom of the list. This seems to be the case with a lot of moms I've talked to. One time I made an appointment for a dental check-up at the dentist I've gone to since I was three. When the dental hygienist looked at my chart as I sat down in the chair, she gasped. "You haven't been here in a year and a half!" she chastised me. As if everybody visits their dentist every six months like clockwork.

"Has it been that long?" I asked, determined not to feel embarrassed by her shock. I'd been to a dental specialist during that time, but evidently that appointment didn't count in her book. I'd never had any major tooth problems previously, but she acted like because of my lapse, all my teeth were going to fall out within weeks.

Later during the appointment, she asked me, "Why was it you went so long without coming in?" Of course, she asked this while all those dental x-ray instruments were in my mouth.

Since my mouth was full, I searched for a short answer to her question. "Ahh ... life," I mumbled. I wished I could hand her a copy of my calendar with all my family's appointments and commitments listed on it.

Life has a way of organizing our priorities for us. Our children are at the top, as they should be, while moms fit in their own schedules when they can. Sure, maybe sometimes we're running late or even running on empty, but we keep on going. That's what moms do. Years ago before boy # three came along, I recall my husband saying something to someone in response to a comment about how busy I was with everything around the house and our boys' schedules plus teaching writing classes. I remember *distinctly* his saying, "Yeah, she's the one who keeps things running around here." That simple statement of recognition—damn near bordering on appreciation—stuck in my mind because it meant so much to me. Of course, now Kevin has no recollection whatsoever of having said that, rendering the compliment and the feeling behind it rather meaningless. Unfortunately, I have no proof and can't remember who he said it to, but trust me—I know he said it. That compliment carried me through many bad days, more so even than the other compliments my husband has given me over the years such as telling me "Hey, you got your figure back" after our first child was born (oddly, he did not say this after the second or third child) or the infamous, "You look fine," given as his stoic, monotone reply for any question I ask him about my appearance.

Yes, moms are charged quite often as being the person who keeps things going in the household. But I have to admit, one time Kevin remembered something that I didn't. I'd misread Jason's baseball tournament brackets and thought he was playing on a Tuesday, but Kevin had heard the coach say after the last practice, "See you Monday." I had been standing there at the practice, too, but I'd missed it. So on Monday afternoon, I had no clue Jason's team was playing that night until Kevin mentioned it. I checked the schedule on-line and wonder of wonders, Kevin was right. He had remembered something instead of me. Folks, this was a big event in our house. A thing of pure amazement. We all stopped doing whatever we were doing and stared at each other. Billy asked me, "Mom, how does it feel to have Dad remember something?" And the truth was it felt good; I liked being able to rely on someone else's memory for once, though I knew not to get used to it because it would probably never happen again. And it didn't.

So with the approach of each new year, I go buy another huge wall to document another 365 days of the O'Donnell family activities. Only now I place it by the computer in our home office instead of by the phone because emails now relay the dates and other information that used to come via phone calls. But I still like to have a wall calendar instead of putting all the dates on my IPhone calendar as many people now do. I like something tangible, the same way I like books made of paper instead of ones on a screen. This decision did come back to haunt me one time when I misread the time of a wedding which we were invited to attend. It was a New Year's Day wedding, and I hadn't put it on the calendar yet because of course, I hadn't yet put up a new wall calendar for the new year. I had been to a shower for the bride-to-be earlier that week, and that time was on that calendar since that was in December. It was at 6:00 pm. And for some reason, that time stuck in my head, making me think the wedding itself was at 6.

But it wasn't. It had been at 5:00. Kevin, David, David's girlfriend, and I found this out the hard way— or at least the embarrassing way—when we walked into the wedding venue where the reception was already going on. We got there at 5:40, thinking we were twenty minutes early. At first, I thought, "Wow, how are they ever going to get all these people milling around to all sit down by 6:00?" I swear, I was clueless. Then a kind friend, suspecting that we'd arrived late, broke it to me gently by saying, "It was a lovely ceremony." I felt physically sick when I heard her words, and in disbelief, I walked over and asked her to repeat what she'd said. Uh-huh. We had missed the whole ceremony. I felt so bad.

Kevin and the boys couldn't believe that reliable mom had messed up so badly. I couldn't either. Billy told me, "That's why you put your schedule in your phone instead of writing it down on some calendar on the wall." Hey, that calendar worked just fine during all your growing up years, buddy.

Part of me wishes I had saved all those calendars so that I could go back and read them—the scribbled notes of appointments and game times, the school project due dates and meetings. A record of our days together as a family. Days when we counted down to vacations. Days when my sons were young. When I look at it like that, keeper of the calendar is not such a bad job after all.

Field Trip Chaperone

Signing up to chaperone field trips is something that parents do to feel they are a part of their children's educational experience. Over the years, I've been on many field trips with my boys from zoos to art museums to tours of the state capitol. One trip that stands out in my mind is when Jason was five, and his pre-school class went to the Museum of Science in downtown Raleigh. I'd signed up to drive, and I knew it was a possibility a teacher might ride with me as one had done in our autumn trip to a corn maze. That meant, of course, I must vacuum out our SUV so the teacher wouldn't be totally appalled upon stepping into our family vehicle. With three sons, I never knew what I'd find when I got in there. Athletic cups and wads of chewed gum were definite possibilities.

I'd planned to take the SUV by one of those auto spa places beforehand and make sure it had a good cleaning. But, as often happens, I never had time to do that. It wasn't until the night before the field trip at bed time that I remembered the car cleaning I'd meant to do. So, I went out into the garage with a flashlight to attempt to do a quick, bare-bones clean-up job. In the interest of time, I decided to focus on the front of the vehicle since the teacher would be sitting up front. I dusted off the seat interior and picked up major items like empty Gatorade bottles, juice boxes, and discarded kid's meal toys. I gathered up dirty socks and DVD boxes (you haven't lived until you drive to Disney while your five-year-old repeatedly watches "The Return of Frosty the Snowman" on the car DVD player).

In the other seats, there were still lots of bits and pieces of trash in the carpet and gunk in the little holes where the seats were adhered to the floor. But the teacher would never see that, just some other five-year-olds who wouldn't notice or care. The front of the SUV looked okay, and I was tired, so I decided to go to bed.

The next day, the plan was to drop off our children as usual and then those driving on the trip would come back an hour later to pick up everybody. When I dropped Jason off, the teacher gave each of the drivers a list of who was riding with them. I scanned the list and stopped cold in my tracks. BOTH teachers were riding with me. Holy cow, that meant one of them would have to sit in *the middle seat.* The middle seat where they would have a perfect angle to see the melted lollipops stuck in the cup holders and sunflower seeds (the 'must-have' snack of all youth baseball players) imbedded in the carpet.

When I got back to my SUV, I jumped in and immediately headed to the self-car wash down the street. I wished I had time to take it to one of those car detailing places, but I didn't. The last time I took our SUV there, the manager inspected every vehicle after the car detail person had finished, ensuring customer satisfaction. I watched as the manager checked off vehicle after vehicle and moved on to the next one. When he came to our SUV, he said, "Hold on there," before they gave me back the keys. "I think we need to do a little more to this one." The poor guy who had cleaned the SUV dropped his head. I was embarrassed for him and for me. After all, the manager didn't see what our SUV had looked like when it first came in; there should be a before and after picture taken of each vehicle so he could see how much work had been done. I told the manager that it looked fine to me, but he insisted on cleaning the seats one more time. I knew my guys were hard on car interiors, dating way back to when we used to have a van when Jason was a baby. Once when I took the van into the car wash, the guy said, and I quote, "Y'all been partying in here!!"

So yes, the SUV needed another car detail job, but that wasn't going to happen that day. I didn't even want to go to an automatic car wash because the last time I did that the big rags hanging down that clean your car stopped completely during the middle of the wash cycle. Since there were cars behind me, I had to go ahead and drivel out of the car wash with soap suds all over my SUV, evident to everyone that I'd screwed up something. I went into the store and got the manager who told me that I hadn't stopped on the right spot, to which I replied that I'd been in plenty of car washes over the years and had always been able to handle it just fine, thank you. He had to let me break in line so that I could rinse my car. So no automation for me again. I pulled into the self-car wash and got to work.

The huge vacuum cleaner there only took quarters but thank God, I had a ton of them at the bottom of my purse. I'd have to work fast. I popped in two quarters and crawled in the back, pulling the enormous vacuum cleaner hose behind me. A few minutes later, the vacuum stopped so I had to climb out and put in two more quarters. After ten minutes of twisting and turning throughout the SUV and squeezing the hose underneath seats, I'd worked up a sweat. But, my work was productive. I found a long-lost athletic cup wedged under the back seat. I sighed, remembering the hour-long search we had for the thing before my middle son's baseball game. It must have fallen out of his equipment bag at some point.

The carpet wasn't totally clean, but it was the best I could do under the circumstances. I pulled out a bottle of cleaner from the back and sprayed it on the sides and backs of the seats, hoping the drips of long-ago dried drinks would come off okay. Some did, some didn't. I looked at my watch and knew I had to get back to the school. I opened all the doors to the vehicle and swung each of them back and forth to air it out so it wouldn't smell like cleaning fluid. I took out some of my middle son's high potency deodorant we kept in the car for times he needed it between events and sprayed it throughout the vehicle.

Then it was off to the school. Both teachers and the kids got into my SUV, and I held my breath as the teacher who climbed in the back seat glanced briefly around as she got in. Her facial expression didn't show disgust so I'd pulled off the impossible. 45 minutes earlier the place was a pigsty.

As we neared the museum, I turned on my blinker to turn into the parking lot only to see a sign saying the lot was full. I suddenly felt nauseated because this meant one thing: parallel parking. Let's suffice it to say that parallel parking is not one of my talents, particularly in the SUV. There are two kinds of people in the world: those who can skillfully and calmly parallel park any vehicle in a small space and those who would do anything to keep from having to parallel park (especially under the watchful eyes of others). I'd be marked off the chaperone list for good. For a moment, I considered dropping everyone in front of the museum, claiming I didn't want them to have to walk too far, and then parking in a lot five blocks away.

But then, there it was: a parking space with some a fair amount of room between it and the car in front. "Oh, there's a good spot," one teacher shouted. I slowed down, as I looked in my rearview mirror and saw nobody was behind me. Was I really going to attempt this?? I'd always been intimidated by the whole concept of parallel parking because obviously with all the backing and turning at specific angles, there was some geometry involved. Yet, the slogan in the Nike commercials popped into my mind: *Just do it.* I pulled beside the car in front of the empty space and backed up, turning the wheel until, to my surprise, the SUV was parked perfectly in the space. Oh my gosh. I felt like a little league baseball outfielder who dives to catch the ball and doesn't realize the ball landed in his glove until the crowd starts cheering.

"Nice job," one teacher said, as I did a double take to make sure I wasn't dreaming. But the SUV was right where it should be and I hadn't hit anything. If I didn't accomplish anything else the rest of the month, that'd be okay; this feeling of achievement was enough to carry me through. I got out of the car, my legs weak, but acted like I parallel parked every day. I stood back and tried to nonchalantly admire my handiwork. If only Kevin could have been there to see this.

The museum that day offered many wonders of nature, but none more amazing that the feat I pulled off. Unfortunately, this occurrence gave me a false sense of confidence in my parking abilities. A few days later, I decided to use my newfound skill again. As I tried to whip the SUV into a parallel space, I almost sideswiped another car on my left. So I gave up and parked farther down the street, leaving the prime parking space for someone braver and more coordinated than I. Obviously, the field trip parallel parking success had been a once in a lifetime thing. I wised up after that and didn't volunteer to drive on field trips if the class was going anywhere parallel parking was a necessity. Wisdom comes with age.

The Drugstore Incident

For many years, my family's nights were always crazy, filled with baseball/basketball practices, Scouts, meetings, and homework assignments. One of the wildest was in the fall of 2007 when I dropped Billy at his calculus tutor's house, which is on the opposite side of town about 30 minutes away. So I had to kill some time until I could go back and pick him up an hour later. Jason was with me, and I'd planned to run some errands. He hadn't been feeling all that great, though, and he ended up falling asleep in the back seat. Which was a terrific excuse not to run errands. I pulled into the parking lot of a Walgreens drug store, got out a book I'd been meaning to read, and settled in. Peace and quiet. Ah.

Then suddenly Jason woke up and said he had to go to the bathroom. He didn't mean pee, either, folks. I could tell by the panic showing on his face that time was of the essence. We raced into Walgreens, and I steered Jason toward the restrooms in the back of the store. By this time, he was walking like a cowboy with hemorrhoids, making it very obvious just what his predicament was.

He finally reached the men's room and went to the bathroom. Again. And again. It was like the Pepto Bismol commercial from hell. I wanted to take him home, but he literally could not leave the toilet. Since there was only one bathroom stall, I stood guard at the door to tell men wanting to go in, "Don't even think about it."

Jason was groaning like a woman in labor. He said, "I keep asking God to help, but it's not working." After about ten minutes, I went to the pharmacy window only to find a long line. I grabbed some Imodium AD chewable tablets, ripped them open, and ran into the men's bathroom. Now I am not the type to open something in a store I haven't paid for. And I always take my cart back where it's supposed to be and not just leave it in the parking lot. But that night, I didn't think twice about ripping open the Imodium AD before paying. I think this is partly because I'd learned from experiences with my older sons that sometimes you can't worry about playing by the rules when you're faced with a dire situation. And this one was dire. D-I-R-E.

"Here, Jason," I said, as I handed him a tablet under the stall door. "Take this. It should make you feel better." He chewed it up, and I went back out to my guard post by the door. The next thing I knew, there was this noise—the unmistakable sound of barfing—from inside the stall. And I still couldn't get him off the toilet.

I called Kevin, who was at David's baseball practice, to tell him to go pick up Billy at the tutor's house. Finally, Jason's stomach calmed down a bit, and I cleaned him up the best I could. I felt guilty about leaving such a mess for someone else to clean up, but I had to get Jason out of there. I wanted to get him home as quickly as possible. I put my arm around Jason and walked briskly to the front of the store to the cashier, with him leaning on me.

"Excuse me," I said to the customer the front of the line. "My son got sick in the bathroom, and I really have a problem here. Could I please go in front of you?" She was very kind and said yes. I told Jason to go stand outside the door so that I could see him because the cool air might make him feel better, and I didn't want him throwing up inside again. I never have cash, so I paid for the Imodium AD with my debit card. Then I got $20 cash back and handed it to the cashier.

"What's this for?" she asked, holding up the $20 bill.

"That's for whoever has to clean up the bathroom," I explained, turning to head out the door.

She protested like a good employee would. "Oh Ma'am, you don't need to do that."

I turned back around, peering at her through tired, groggy eyes and said, "You haven't seen the bathroom." She and the other people in line laughed as I turned to go out. "And you might want to put a sign on the men's door," I added. Hell, I thought, they'd probably cordon it off with yellow crime scene tape. I can only trust the cashier didn't pocket the $20 while someone else had to clean up the bathroom. I hope nobody got fired for refusing to clean it up. Just to be on the safe side, we no longer go to that particular Walgreens in case someone who worked there that fateful night might be working again and remember us. If we should ever venture to that side of town again and happen to go in there again, I can just hear the manager sending out a special alert on his walkie-talkie: "All employees, code red! Repeat code red! Quick, lock the bathroom doors!" Other drug stores probably heard about the incident and all have instituted special employee training to deal with such possible situations in the future. Can you say, "No ma'am, we have no public restrooms"?

May Contain Peanuts

I used to associate allergies primarily with pollen season. In my limited view, allergies seemed to be nothing more than an inconvenience that could be alleviated with medication. With the birth of Jason, however, I got a crash course in the reality of allergies. He had dry skin as soon as he was born, but I didn't immediately attribute it to allergies.

Then came the night when Jason was eight months old and our family went out to eat with some friends of ours who also had a baby. When it was time for dessert, the other child's parents let their baby try some spoonfuls of vanilla ice cream, which he loved. We were tempted to give Jason a taste, too, since he'd been on breast milk and a formula supplement so long and might enjoy a treat for his young taste buds. So we gave him a small spoonful. He loved it. We gave him a little more. All of a sudden, he began to throw up all the ice cream and then broke out in hives. Quickly, we gathered up our diaper bag, cups of Cheerios, and teething toys and left the restaurant. I turned and surveyed the mess we were leaving behind. "Leave a big tip," I whispered to Kevin.

Soon after that, we took Jason to an allergist. The doctor pricked Jason's back with some common allergens to see what the reaction would be. I watched with alarm as three red welts as huge as big mosquito bites appeared on Jason's fair skin, signaling the presence of severe food allergies. It's never a good sign when the doctor is so impressed with the extent of the reaction that he calls in the nurses and other doctors to take a look. But that's what happened to us. No milk, eggs, or peanuts for Jason. So I began to carefully monitor what he ate, standing in the grocery store aisles scouring ingredient labels. I became very familiar with the phrase, "May Contain Peanuts", which is printed on almost all of the packaged food made. What's with these food companies? Either say it does have peanuts or it doesn't but don't leave us parents guessing and having to avoid lots of food that might really be safe. I realize they don't want to take any risks and want to avoid law suits, but come on. Peanuts can't possibly have come in contact with every blankin' food product in the universe!

I'd read that sometimes kids get such allergies through something that happened during pregnancy; I started to feel really guilty about the three weeks when I was pregnant with Jason that I had cravings for banana, raisin, and peanut butter sandwiches on whole wheat. Maybe if I hadn't eaten those, Jason wouldn't be allergic to peanuts. With Billy, I'd craved Picante sauce and with David it was asparagus and ginger salad dressing (when I used to go by the Kanki Japanese restaurant just to buy bottles of their ginger dressing). Why couldn't I have stuck with one of those with Jason instead of eating peanut butter?

Jason also tested positive to certain mold spores and dust mites, both of which are hard to monitor or control. I was particularly disheartened about the dust mites allergy because dusting is not something I do often in my house, and I hated to think my lack of housecleaning would harm my son. He would break out in a rash and get itchy often, and he had a number of medicines he took to help lessen this. Yet, it was still a frustrating battle.

For his first birthday, I wanted Jason to have a real cake with creamy, yummy frosting. What's a birthday without a cake? Luckily, I found a bakery that makes a delicious dairy-free chocolate cake (thank you Blue Moon Bakery). I can only imagine how Jason felt as he licked his frosting-covered fingers for the first time and then liking it so much, leaned his head over and took a big bite right out of the cake.

His skin problems were diagnosed as eczema, which often goes hand-in-hand with allergies. I've gone through dozens of creams and ointments that sometimes helped, but never cured, his rashes. He was on Singulair and Zyrtec at one time, then switched to Claritin and then to Allegra, all while also having an inhaler and nose spray, which is part of the reason we were at the pharmacy all the time. Add in the medications for the rest of us, and the place was our home away from home. One time when I dropped off yet another prescription to be filled, one of the staff pharmacists asked me the routine question, "Have you been here before?"

"You've gotta be kidding me," I replied. "With the amount of money we've spent here, we've practically put your kids through college."

When Jason was a baby, the itching made his already poor sleep patterns even worse. Therefore, it was really difficult to change Jason's sleep habits like we did with our older boys by putting them in the crib and letting them cry while we periodically checked on them until they fell asleep after an hour or so (the famous 'let them cry it out' method). This method is supposed to teach them to go to sleep on their own and to stay asleep. With Jason, I always felt guilty for letting him cry because his eyes and skin would get more inflamed the more he cried, causing me to throw in the towel and pick him up.

Finally, there was a day when he was about ten months old when his eyes and skin were clear so I decided to let him do the 'crying thing' for a while. I'd go in to check on him and reassure him, gradually increasing the increments of time between the checks. He was so tired I was sure it wouldn't take long for him to fall asleep.

Four hours later, he was still crying. I don't know how he did it. Superman in diapers. The rest of our family was a nervous wreck. Miraculously, he eventually closed his eyes and drifted off to sleep. "Ahhh," I thought, "He's down for the count." Thirty-five minutes later he was awake again, smiling and ready to play.

Winner and still champion.

When Jason was four, I enrolled him in an egg allergy study at Duke, and we had to make the 30 minute trip twice a month. One day as we drove into Durham, he played quietly with his toys in his car seat, as I made a mental note of my 'to do' list. For once, we were actually running on time, and I sighed, contentedly. We were leaving on vacation the next day, and we were all packed and ready. After this appointment, there would be a few small errands, and then the day would be done.

Suddenly, there was a whooshing vacuum sound from the back seat. I turned quickly, thinking I'd blown a tire. At the same time, Jason let out an ear-piercing scream and threw something into the air that landed on the other side of the car. "What did you do?" I yelled, my heart climbing in to my throat as I struggled to look at him and keep the car in my lane.

Then I saw the blood on his fingers. I knew then what it was he'd thrown into the air: it was his Epi-Pen shot needle, one of several we have at various places in case he should ever have a severe reaction to peanuts and need epinephrine immediately. In addition to the one at home and at pre-school, we also carried one in his bag which contained a change of clothes and toys but also a medicine pouch on the side, which he had never shown an interest in before. The Epi-Pen was in a sealed round, clear container inside a sealed cardboard box, which was inside a sealed plastic bag inside the zipped medicine pouch. Yet, Jason had managed to get it out without my ever suspecting anything. He, who became frustrated trying to get a Popsicle out of its wrapper, now was adept at going through three barriers to obtain an object without so much as a whine or a "Mom, can you get this open for me?"

I leaned back toward his car seat and pressed my right thumb tightly over the bloody area on his hand, all while driving with my left hand and watching the road. I was already headed to Duke and was only five minutes away, so I decided to keep going; they knew all his allergy information there anyway. Still, I'd have to park in the mega-level parking deck and take Jason all the way to the clinic in my arms. I knew the Epi-Pen could possibly save his life someday, but I'd never thought to ask what would happen if he got a dose of it when he didn't need it. Probably nothing, I told myself to keep me calm.

"I'm so sorry," I told a still-screaming Jason in as soothing of a voice as I could manage. "That was my fault, not yours. I shouldn't have had that in the bag." I lifted my thumb briefly and glanced at his hand. The bleeding had stopped, but I still kept the pressure applied. "It's okay," I assured him.

As I took the Duke exit off of the interstate, Jason's crying finally subsided. Then he mumbled, "I'm so sleepy, Mommy." Jason is never sleepy, not even at midnight. Concerned, I took a quick look at him. His eyes were rolling back in his head, and he was suddenly too drowsy to carry on conversation.

My heart rate sped up again, and I floored the accelerator, speaking loudly to tell Jason not to go to sleep. I patted his hand, his face, to rouse him. I sped down the street to the parking garage, where I found a parking place on the third level. I jumped out and grabbed Jason, threw him over my shoulder. Then I got his bag of toys that we usually took to his appointments and even had the presence of mind to get the needle he had used so it could be examined. I was no novice at this mom thing.

Then the race was on. Duke is a big place, and running with a forty pound child on one's shoulders is not an easy task. My adrenalin must have kicked in, though. I ran to the elevators with Jason and the heavy bag, got to the second floor, raced through the bridge that carries people over the street, ran down another long hallway, passed the escalators, and went through two sets of double doors, until I finally burst into the clinic. It was like an action scene out of one of those emergency room TV dramas. The nurses were waiting to see Jason for his regularly scheduled appointment, so luckily, they were all right there when we pushed open the door.

I rushed in, saying almost out of breath, "Jason gave himself an Epi-Pen shot in the car. He got really sleepy all of a sudden so I've been trying to keep him awake."

"He's so pale," one of the nurses said. They put Jason on a bed and took his blood pressure, which was normal. A nurse got on the phone to Jason's allergist at Duke who told us that the medicine would have made Jason hyper, not sleepy. They decided that it was the shock and crying that had worn Jason out so quickly and made him want to go to sleep. I remembered something similar had happened years earlier to David when he shut his finger in the car door, cried uncontrollably, and then fell asleep five minutes later. Maybe shock *was* the reason. I breathed a sigh of relief.

The doctor also said that although the needle had expended the full dose, Jason probably didn't get much of the medicine in his system because he had immediately thrown the needle into the air. The needle had punctured Jason's thumb so we needed to make certain blood flow wasn't cut off to that area.

They called ahead to the ER and told them we were on our way. Jason and I sat in a wheelchair as a nurse pushed us through the meandering labyrinth of the hospital hallways. At the ER, they monitored him for a few hours, and pretty soon, he was back to his old self, thank goodness. I tried repeatedly to call Kevin but couldn't reach him.

As we got in the car to go home after our long afternoon, Jason told me, shaking his head back and forth, "I'll never, ever, mess with my medicine again." I leaned over and hugged him, saying a silent prayer of thanks that he was okay.

As I drove away I thought about how I threw Jason over my shoulder and ran through the hospital like O.J. Simpson used to run through airports. Moms really don't know what kind of strength and stamina they have until their child is in trouble. When we got back home, I pulled into the driveway just as Kevin was driving in, too. I'd not been able to contact him so he still didn't know what had happened. He got out of the car with his gym bag in hand, obviously having just finished working out. He stretched and said, "Whew, I've had a tough day."

I eyed the gym bag with disdain. "I tried to call you to let you know Jason was in the ER, but I guess you don't get coverage at the Y," I told him. He looked at me, alarmed.

Jason ran past yelling, "I got to ride in a wheelchair, Dad!" I then told all the details of the afternoon to a concerned Kevin, who very wisely asked at the end of the conversation, "You want to go out to eat tonight instead of making dinner??"

That would be a yes.

Ode to the Laundry Room

An ode is written in honor of something, a way to sing the praises of something. Thus, I call this an ode to the laundry room as in praise of the *concept* of laundry rooms, but I myself don't have one. Not having one makes me realize how praiseworthy laundry rooms really are.

When my husband and I bought our house 28 years ago, we didn't have children yet. At that point, laundry day was just that: ONE day a week to get caught up on washing, drying, and maybe a little ironing. So when the realtor said to us, "And the washer and dryer are upstairs behind these bi-fold doors, and people love upstairs laundry facilities," we smiled and nodded our heads in approval. Our bedrooms were upstairs, so that would be convenient. We were oblivious to the fact that there was a huge difference in upstairs laundry rooms and simply upstairs washers and dryers behind bi-fold doors at the top of the stairs.

It was convenient for a year or so. Until we had son number 1. After his birth and a sudden increase in dirty clothes and a decrease of our time to spend on laundry, there were some warning signs of what was to come. Our laundry day quickly became several laundry days which soon became a never-ending week-long event. I don't remember it, but I know there was the day I first pulled the clothes out of the dryer and left them lying there in a pile at the top of our stairs. Maybe I was in a hurry—the baby was crying or it was the middle of the night and I was washing soiled crib sheets. It all blurred together. And the next thing I knew, laundry would magically accumulate in unfolded piles beside the dryer. The problem was this area was at the top of our balcony landing that looks down into our foyer. It's not aesthetically pleasing to see a sock hanging down through the balcony railing beside the chandelier.

When the second son came along, the laundry volume grew exponentially. As the piles of clothes in our balcony area grew to mounds, I knew we had a definite problem. This little area would become, by necessity, a makeshift laundry room. Only this laundry room didn't have a door we could close to hide it all. Then there came a time that I first uttered those infamous words when the boys' friends would come over: "Just step over the clothes at the top of the stairs!" Soon, it was like second nature to them; their friends jumped over and maneuvered around the mounds of clothes like they didn't even notice them. It was just a part of the O'Donnell household.

When the third son was born, things really got complicated. Before him, I used to actually fold the clothes sooner or later and put them in the appropriate drawers or closets. But after the third one, the effects of lack of sleep set in. I just began to throw the items of clothing toward the correct son's room, and if it landed in the general area in front of their door—well then, bull's eye. My middle son started playing baseball in the spring, summer, and fall, and baseball uniforms are extremely difficult to clean due to the ground-in mud and grass stains, particularly if he were to slide and got mud caked on his pants. This led to a whole array of spray cleaners and bleach sticks added to our little laundry area and lots of time spent trying repeatedly to scrub out these stains.

Now before all of you start asking why my sons didn't do the laundry, let me say that they did. Ever since Billy was a senior in high school, he kept all of his own laundry separate and did it himself. David did his in high school sometimes, but ever since that incident when his new wool sweater 'somehow' got in the dryer, I'd rather keep his participation to a minimum. Of course, once in college, he started his laundry and never brought any home. There was that one ironing incident when he was in Boston for an internship, and he thought he could go use the bathroom while the iron sat face-down on his nice gray suit pants. Nope! The pants had a triangular-shaped brown scorch mark and were totally ruined. So glad he didn't burn down the hotel.

And Jason has done a pretty good job of starting washer and dryer loads, even if he does leave the folded clothes in piles on the floor surrounding the bi-fold doors. Clothes in piles do get wrinkled if you don't get to them soon enough, particularly when our long-haired dachshund burrows down into them to make a cozy place to take a nap. Attempting to find a solution to the wrinkled clothes problem, I bought a clothes steamer several years ago so that I wouldn't have to pull out the ironing board (no place to leave it up and I'm not about to have that permanently at the top of our stairs). This works pretty well, but it looks like a huge IV pole. I like to think it gives our bedroom character.

In the past year, we had to get a new washer and dryer, and I talked my husband into buying one of those driers with the steam cycle in it. Love, love, love this! Just throw a few wrinkled items inside and hit 'refresh' or 'wrinkle care'. The washer is one of those "high efficiency" ones that requires a special kind of detergent with "HE" on the front of the box. The irony in having HE on the washer is not lost on me, when so much of the laundry chores are done by a SHE.

As good as my new washer and dryer are, though, they are still behind those blasted bi-fold doors at the top of the stairs. Of course, I'm thankful to have a washer and dryer at all. Whenever one of them is broken, I have seen what it's like to have to transport all our stuff to a laundromat and back. Still, I can dream of a laundry room. I daydreamed about it again last week when the guys from Sears came to deliver a new mattress for my son. In order for them to get it safely into his room, I had to make sure the area at the top of the stairs was free of clothes and laundry baskets. When I'd moved and picked up everything, I walked back around the corner and saw the empty space where it all had been, and it damn near took my breath away. We had hardwood floors under there! I had forgotten. Maybe, I thought to myself, we could keep it just like that and make sure all the clothes are folded and put away right as they come out of the dryer. Sure it would be a continuous, nonstop ordeal, but we could do it. And then I'd come back down to reality. Nope, the area at the top of the stairs would always have clothes all over it—folded, unfolded, in piles, hanging to dry from door tops. This was indeed my laundry 'room.' But maybe someday ...

Mom by the Pool

Swimming and summer, of course, go hand-in-hand. All my boys have taken swim lessons over the years at the local YMCA. They always liked me to watch their classes and see the improvements they made during class. I'd give them the thumbs-up sign to encourage them and pay close attention because they would inevitably ask me afterwards, "Mom, did you see me when I dove off the side?" The few times Kevin took one of them, he'd use the time to take a nap; the boys would come home telling on their dad: "Mom, dad fell asleep at my swim lessons!" As if that was something I didn't expect.

With Billy and David, I would usually wear my swim suit, too, so that I could get a little sun while I waited for them. Being an older mom with Jason, I'd forego the whole swim suit thing with him and just wear shorts because getting more sun would eventually only make me look like an older 'older' mom. With Jason, I decided to let comfort win out over style. A mom of a certain age has earned the right to wear baggy shorts and flip-flops at the pool just like the dads wear. That is truly women's liberation.

And if I did decide to wear an actual bathing suit when I took Jason to the pool, it was the bathing suit with the skirt rather than two-piece that I chose when I was a 30-something mom. I was also the mom with a towel over her face to avoid more age spots. A mom with age gap children gets more laid-back about things with our youngest child than we were with our older children. The younger moms at the pool would bring snacks from home for their children—coolers of fresh fruit and veggies, and even gag—kale chips—while I would scrounge around in the bottom of my purse so Jason could buy a hot dog.

Going to the pool with the guys was never a favorite thing of mine even when I was young; I've never been cut out to be a pool kind of mom, though a lot of that has to do with that fact that my naturally curly hair frizzes badly in the summer humidity and Lord help me if I were to go into the pool to cool off and let my hair dry naturally. I remember how nervous I was when each of the guys started lessons as pre-schoolers; I'd sit as close to the poolside as I could so I could jump in and save them in case something should go wrong, forgetting that I myself was not a good swimmer in the first place.

All my boys became good swimmers, and I was happy about that, especially because of my own lack of swimming skill. Oh, I could dog paddle with the best of 'em. I even passed the swim test that my university had all of its students take as a graduation requirement. But I was never one of those kids who could cut through the water like a fish and play games retrieving pennies from the deep end of the pool. I always wanted to be.

Swim lessons have gotten better since I was a kid. When I took them one summer at a local college, rumor had it that everyone would be forced to jump off the super high diving board at the end of the week. This diving board was the mother of all diving boards, so high that it almost touched the ceiling of the huge indoor facility. To make matters worse, the class had about 20 kids in it with one instructor who barked out commands instead of demonstrating on a one—on-one basis. When we had to use kick boards and kick ourselves across the pool, I was behind everyone and got so much water in my face that I started coughing and sputtering. I'll never forget my poor mother standing up in the stands and yelling, "Get Sharon!" I'm sure that was a proud moment for her.

Afterwards, I found out that the cutest boy in the whole fourth grade was in the swim class right after mine and had seen the whole episode. This is the same boy that I once ran into at a dime store right after my hair had dried really frizzy after swimming, so I hid behind a beach ball display the whole time our mothers talked. Can we say 'conspicuous'? I wasn't about to make a fool of myself in front of him yet again. I was so embarrassed that I quit swim lessons, never even finding out if The Rumor about the high dive was true or not.

So I was happy when Billy took swim lessons at the YMCA and turned out to be a pretty good swimmer by the time he was six. It was a good thing too. When David was three, we were at a water park in New Hampshire, and he and I were in one of those wave pools on an inner tube. Six-year-old Billy had his own tube, and Kevin had gone to get something out of our locker. I was relaxing, bobbing up and down on the water with David, not paying a lot of attention to anything when suddenly the tsunami of all water park waves came barreling toward David and me. I felt like we were in a sequel to *The Perfect Storm*. The tsunami wave broke over us and flipped the inner tube over, throwing me backwards into the shallow water and onto the concrete below. I surfaced, hearing shrieks and screams all around me. I looked frantically around for David. And there he was standing on the other side of the shallow end beside his big brother, Billy, thank God. "Wow!" Billy yelled, "That was a big one!"

One of the cute teen guys who worked there hurried over to me to make sure I was all right. "I saw you get hit pretty hard," he said. My knee and arm were a little skinned up and bloodied, but that was it, other than an extremely wounded pride. Not exactly a perfect day at the water park. I wanted to ask if the wave machine had gone a little wild or something, but I didn't have the energy. An equipment malfunction or something? I took David by the hand and walked out of the pool, blood trickling down my elbow and knee.

About that time, Kevin came back from the locker room and stared at me as he walked up. "What in the world happened to you?" he asked.

"That was *not* a normal wave," I told him. "And here's David." I put David's hand in Kevin's and made it back to the sandy beach area where I managed to crawl up onto a chair and collapse in a heap, covering my wounded self with a towel. The flesh-toned Band-Aids looked lovely on my knees.

Falling Asleep
on September 11th

I found out about the September 11th terrorist attacks while I was teaching writing to students at an elementary school. As I was teaching, I noticed the principal come into the classroom and speak in hushed tones with the teacher, but I had no idea the magnitude of what they were whispering about. At the end of class, the teacher came up to me, a solemn look on her face, and broke the unbelievable news. A strange feeling arose in my stomach like someone had just knocked all the breath out of me.

It was time for my break, and I'd arranged to meet my friend Robyn for brunch before heading back to teach another writing class. Before I drove to meet her, however, I sat in the school parking lot, listening to the news coverage, my heart becoming heavy—literally—with grief. Without a television nearby, I hadn't yet seen the horrifying video of the planes crashing into the World Trade Centers. It was impossible to imagine. I thought of the photo on my refrigerator—the one taken on a New York City trip three years earlier when my two oldest boys were ages seven and four. I took it of them as we crossed the water going to the Statue of Liberty. They're bundled in their sweaters, grinning. The skyline of New York is behind them, the World Trade Towers hovering over it all, standing tall and majestic in the background. Billy, who was really into skyscrapers at the time, kept yelling, "Make sure you have the towers in the picture!"

I went to meet Robyn for brunch, but neither of us felt like eating any more. So we sat and talked, sharing our pain, our fear, how vulnerable we felt. We each had three young children, and we couldn't help but ask ourselves "What next? Where next? Who next?" Questions that would continue to plague our minds, our souls.

As I entered the school after my break, I walked underneath the flagpole with the American flag flying high, flapping in the breeze above. Shielding my eyes from the sun, I looked up at the flag that suddenly meant even more to me than it had just an hour or so before. Still proud, still free. Still America. Then I went into the classroom full of fourth graders and looked out at their faces—faces filled with innocence and hope and trust. Biting my lip, I said a silent prayer that this world wouldn't let them down.

When I got home that afternoon, I took down the New York vacation photo from the refrigerator and placed my hand over the Trade Towers, trying to imagine the city without them. It became an unfamiliar city skyline. Then I watched the news as it showed President Bush's deliberate walk into the White House for the first time since it had all happened. The world waited for his words, his response. "Be with him, God," I mumbled as I marveled at the weight of the burden he must be carrying.

That night I lay in between David and Billy, 7 & 10, as they went to sleep in the same bed instead of their separate ones as usual. When he was younger, David used to pinch my arm while he drifted off to sleep. He hadn't done that in quite some time. But that night I felt his small hand touch my upper arm and lightly pinch it repeatedly as he fell asleep. I closed my eyes & sighed, wondering what dreams would fill my children's heads during the night. I pulled both boys closer to me, and the three of us lay there in the dark, the night quiet around us. Warm, secure, safe. I wished we could stay like that forever.

IV
A Woman of a Certain Age

An archaeologist is the best husband any woman can have: the older she gets, the more interested he is in her.

—Agatha Christie

Author note: Obviously Agatha didn't consider how awesome it would be to have a top-notch plastic surgeon as a husband.

Where the Hell Did That Come From?

Silly me. I'd thought that once the kids were all older, I'd simply pick back up where I'd left off as if nothing had changed. As if *I* hadn't changed. As if my body hadn't changed. Holy cow. I had my first son at age 29, my second at 32, and my third and last at age 38. By the time my youngest turned seven and could do a lot of things independently, I realized I was 45. Five years to go until 50, and I suddenly thought "Stop this ride, I want to get off!" Where had the time gone? More specifically, where had *MY* time gone?? When I turned 55, I had to say the age out loud to try to make it sink in. And I still had a son in high school. I really was feeling like an older mom.

Being an older mom, it is only natural for me to compare what I feel like with my third son to what I felt like with my first two sons. The pregnancies weren't a lot different except for two things: older moms can't possibly ever look cute in maternity clothes, and I had to have more ultrasounds due to my age. With all three of my pregnancies, I took folic acid during pregnancy & even when I was simply *trying* to become pregnant because I know it reduces the possibility of birth defects; with my third child, I was even more diligent about it since the older the mom, the higher the risk of birth defects.

The years after the pregnancy have been different in the sense that I'm viewed differently. I was no longer a 30 something mom with two little boys; I was one of those moms in her late 40s-early 50s with one child considerably younger than the other two, a mom who had been there and done that with the first two and was in the midst of round three. It's also been different because my husband and I are generally more laid-back with parenthood the third time around, so we don't worry as much about the small things.

Yet, I have to say the biggest challenge with being an older mom is simply the getting older part. I'm a mom, yes, but I'm also a woman who worries about crow's feet and extra pounds. Having a younger child has made these growing older years for me more of a challenge because I'm still dealing with my child's needs rather than finally being able to concentrate on me once again. And that's okay: that's what a mom does, and I'd have it no other way. But it certainly causes me to dwell on that getting older part.

Instead of picking back up where I left off before I had kids, I realized I was falling apart. It wasn't that I could say I raised my kids and now it was my time; it was that I raised my kids and suddenly I wasn't me anymore. Not emotionally and certainly not physically. The late Nora Ephron had a bestselling book about aging called "I Feel Bad About My Neck." She was able to actually select *one* body part that she felt bad about for her book title. I would never be able to choose. I'd have to call the book, "I Feel Bad About My Whole Friggin' Body".

I remember the night I was breastfeeding my third son on the couch when he was two months old. I sat back and sighed in contentment while I watched TV, while resting my left arm on—what the hell was that I was resting my arm on? I looked down only to discover I was resting my arm on a roll of flab around my middle! Where the hell did that come from? And more importantly, I thought, how do I make it disappear? This hadn't happened after I had my first two sons. Was this some kind of Third Baby Fat Curse or something? Since then, I've lost some of that roll but not all of it, and what is left is stubborn and seems to have settled in for the long haul.

Personal dreams and goals have to still be a part of an older mom's life, and my dream has always been to be a writer. However, being a writer is not conducive to getting back in shape. Say if my goal in life was not to write books but to be an Olympic swimmer or volleyball player, then pursuing that dream could have been done simultaneously with keeping in shape; instead I've spent countless hours at the computer, which has resulted in extra pounds and back surgery, which is another story. If God planted the dream in me of being a writer, then I think He should at least be a little lenient on the roll of flab thing.

Okay, let's move on to another body part, shall we? The face. Ah, the face, which has inspired poets to write many verses of rhyme. When a woman enters her mid-40s, she becomes increasingly aware of those apostrophe-shaped lines on the sides of her nose. Just as she begins to accept those, lo and behold, more little apostrophe lines appear only this time they show up on both sides of her mouth. The proper name for these is 'marionette lines', which sounds way too pretty to describe these dastardly little wrinkles. These are so called because they resemble the lines which enable a Marionette puppet mouth to open and close. It was good to finally have an official name of the thing I detested so much.

I remember distinctly the morning I made the alarming discovery of my first marionette lines. It was July 15, 2007. Approximately 7:15 a.m. I went to bed without the wrinkles and woke up with them. That fateful morning I was brushing my teeth in front of the bathroom mirror when I froze, my toothbrush stopped in mid-brush, staring in horror at my face. And once more I asked that phrase, "Where the hell did *that* come from?" These are words that women over 45 will mutter to themselves or sometimes scream out loud throughout the rest of their lives. Ladies, have we paid our dues yet for Eve eating that apple? I should think so.

Sometimes I'll say to my sons, "Look," while I pull the sides of my mouth up with my fingers and raise my eyebrows, creating a younger, smoother face by stretching my skin upwards.

"What?" they'll ask, totally unimpressed.

"Look how much better my face looks like this," I'll say. "Doesn't it?" They won't answer, just roll their eyes or shake their heads because they don't know that at this stage in my life I need a little confidence, a little reassurance. My God, guys, I need some damn compliments. Instead I get NOTHING from my husband and oldest boys and undesired complete and total honesty from my youngest son. In 2011, I was driving with Jason in the passenger seat, and I noticed that he was staring at me. "What is it?" I asked.

"Nothing," he replied and tried to dismiss it.

I, like a dummy, pressed the issue. "Really, what is it?"

"Well, you have, like, lines on the side of your eye."

"Those are wrinkles, honey," I said as sweet as I could, resisting the urge to stop and make him get out of the car and walk home.

Okay. Next body part. Let's zoom in on the eyes. Several years ago, I began to notice that my eyelashes weren't as long as they used to be, and I'd gaze at girls with those long lashes and wonder what kind of mascara they used. I tried all the different brands until one day, I realized the truth: mascara had nothing to do with it. My lashes looked shorter because my eyelids were drooping. Damn. Another body part bites the dust. As of yet, the only improvement surgery I've had was Lasik surgery for my eyesight back in 2001, and that has been wonderful. I'll definitely take clear vision over an eyelid lift any day. Well, almost any day.

My oldest son had eyelid surgery when he was 25 to make his eyes close completely when he sleeps rather than having that tiny part of his eye showing since this contributed to dry eye problems. Let me repeat that: my son was going to get to have eyelid surgery before I would. Some things in this world just aren't fair.

I recently discovered there is this really cool relatively new 'procedure' called a Mommy Makeover. The one I read about consisted of a tummy tuck, boob lift, and some tightening of abdominal muscles. I am all over that. A Mommy Makeover sounds divine. They market it brilliantly, saying that moms deserve to get back the body they had before kids. It's not like plastic surgery for celebrities or anything vain; it is simply moms getting back what they lost during pregnancy and motherhood. Hey, boys, if you are ever at a loss as to what to give me for Mother's Day, I have a suggestion for you.

Being a woman over 45 is tough, no doubt about it. Even more so when that woman is an older mom. It has gotten to the point that there are way too many things to do to myself at nighttime before going to bed—lotions, moisturizers, ointments, vitamins and such. Moms are so tired at night that there is no way they can take care of themselves the way they are supposed to; and, the older the mom, the more there is to take care of. It's gotten to the point that I put off going to bed because I don't feel like going through it all. And I haven't even mentioned osteoporosis or pelvic floor problems—more things to look forward to. Or menopause with hot flashes and new chemical imbalances.

Yes, when a woman reaches a certain age, she will notice inexplicable things about her body and face that change literally overnight. She will be trying on clothes in one of those dressing rooms with mirrors on all the walls providing kind of a 3-D experience and will start hyperventilating when she catches a glimpse of her knees which suddenly seem to have no shape to them at all. What happened to the dang kneecap? It seems to have turned into fold after fold of nothing but skin. And she wonders if she really should order Crepe Erase cream even though it looks too good to be true. She never thought she'd worry about her knees of all things. But you don't really appreciate them until they're gone. Which pretty much is life's lesson about everything, especially for women.

We endure the periods, we go through pregnancy and labor, and raising the kids and then just as there is a bit of light at the end of the tunnel, we physically fall apart. I recall the day when I was 47 when my doctor informed me in a bit too cheerful of a voice, "Your uterus has dropped and is pressing on your bladder." Uhmm ... yeah, I could have told you that. I'd been feeling like my insides were about to fall out for the past five years. "It's those three big boys you had," she laughed. She then told me if it gets too bad, then I can have surgery. But what is considered 'too bad"? I had back surgery in 2008 and don't want to have anything else unless it's absolutely necessary (or of course unless it's a face or eye lift). A lot of women feel the same way about unneeded surgery, and so there are a lot of us out there putting up with uncomfortable stuff like dropped uteruses. Or is that uteri? Anyway, some mind-boggling things happen to a woman's 'innards' when she gets to be a certain age, especially if she's had kids. You will know it when you feel it. Trust me.

Sometimes I do fantasize about eyelifts or facelifts. Alas, the only time I've been able to visit a plastic surgeon was when I had to have a knot taken off the side of my arm. My plastic surgeon (those 3 words together makes me giddy!) was a nice enough guy, but I'm not sure he realized how his words came across to me. He and his nurse started talking about a micro-dermabrasion treatment that she'd had recently at a related facility nearby. Feeling like I should join in the conversation, I asked about the procedure, which led to my doctor pointing to a mole under my left eye and asking, "Is that like a beauty mark or something?" From the way he said it, I could tell he thought it was more like the 'something' than a beauty mark.

"Well," I began, "people used to call it a beauty mark when it was just a dark freckle under my eye, but over the years it's just become pretty much a mole. But the dermatologist said that it's a good mole and has no signs of cancer. So I've never seriously thought about taking it off."

Still staring at my mole, the doctor replied, "That's the first thing I'd do to your face." The FIRST thing??? I'd been in his office 10 minutes, and the man had a *list!* I didn't dare ask what the second thing would be. I felt my self-esteem deflating and was amazed there wasn't a gushing air sound surrounding me as all of my confidence was pulled out of me and into space—kind of like in the *Space Jam* movie when the aliens sucked all the talent out of the basketball stars. Since I am a mom of boys, that is the image that popped into my head.

I took a deep breath and tried to appear unfazed. "But my dermatologist said if he took it off, it would leave a scar more noticeable than the mole itself," I offered.

The surgeon was about to walk out the door but turned and glanced at me again. "No, no, it would be fine because you have enough wrinkles that it wouldn't matter."

Whoa. Now that was a low blow. He and his nurse exchanged a quick look between them, and even he realized it. He smiled. "I'm not saying you have a lot of wrinkles, it's just that you have enough that a small scar wouldn't be noticeable." I don't even remember my response, but I think I just smiled and nodded. Quite frankly, I just wanted him to STOP TALKING. Please God, stop the man from talking.

And yes, I'm sure there will be many more times to come when I will look into a mirror and yell, "Where the hell did *that* come from?"

The Reunions

Trying to look halfway decent at high school reunions is also one of life's challenges when you reach a certain age. Luckily, I've really enjoyed my high school reunions because of course everybody is the same age: we're all struggling with the same things, creating kind of a bond between us, even between the popular ones and geeky ones from back then. The years that have gone by give you more empathy for others and have taught you that you and your classmates have lots more in common than things that set you apart.

But damn it, you still want to look good without it being obvious that you are trying to look good. You know what I mean?

What's tough is when you attend events where you haven't seen someone in a while, and younger women are there, too. About ten years ago, two of my best friends and college buddies, Amy and Michelle, and I attended a gathering of the local alumni chapter of the sorority we'd belonged to at UNC-Chapel Hill. The three of us met in the parking lot of the On the Border restaurant where the meeting was taking place. The meeting organizer had sent out a note saying to look for the trademark black and gold balloons of Kappa Alpha Theta at the table. We were nervous because we didn't know who we would see there, especially since we hadn't kept in touch with anyone but each other over the past 23 years. We decided to go into the restaurant and walk toward the balloons but to quickly abort the mission and switch to plan B if for some reason we chickened out and didn't want to go to the sorority table. I took along photos of my kids, prepared to say my usual response to the age gap comment, "Yes, I did space them out a lot, didn't I?" As the hostess greeted us, we spotted the balloons flying high above a table far back in the corner to our right. We told her we were meeting someone already there and proceeded to walk cautiously toward the balloons. As we got closer, we saw that all the women at the table seemed to be at least ten years younger than us. "Abort, abort!" Amy said in a loud whisper. "Go left!" The three of us veered away from the balloon table and toward the women's restroom where we regrouped and soon got a table of our own away from the younger Theta women who would probably be carded if they ordered a margarita. Alumni? Give me a break. When did they graduate? Last month?

The most recent high school reunion I attended was a different kind of reunion. Instead of being just our class, the organizers invited 13 classes for a multi-class reunion. The classes of 1979 through 1992 were invited. I was in the Class of 1980. This meant that there would be women 12 years younger than I was at this class reunion! Are you kidding me? As I mentioned earlier, part of the comfort of a class reunion is knowing that everyone is the same age, going through similar physical things. But 55-year-olds going to a class reunion with 43-year-olds? Being older than most of the people there? Sure! Sounds like a fun night. Actually, it wasn't too bad, and it was nice to see the handful of my classmates who showed up, as well as a few people I knew from some of the other classes. But I didn't ever get on the dance floor because the nerve problem in my right foot made my toes go numb. Crap. I really do sound old.

Spanx Adventures

After my 25th high school reunion, I promised myself that I would never again wear any type garment designed to hold in or push in fat in order to make me look thinner. The dynamics of it just doesn't work out. If fat is pushed from somewhere, then logically it has to show up somewhere else, right? And I spent way too much time in the bathroom trying to roll back up garments that were rolling down when they weren't supposed to be. But that was before I had heard of Spanx. When Spanx came out, it was all the rage in Hollywood, and all the stars were raving about it. I'd even heard people I know praise Spanx.

So one day when I was 49, I decided to buy some Spanx to wear under a dress I was going to wear to a wedding. I was more than a bit self-conscious about going to buy the Spanx in a store, but I knew to get the right size that I needed to do so rather than ordering on line. I found a department store that had a good selection of Spanx along with a video of an Oprah show where guests were talking about it and how wonderful it is. However, I didn't want anyone to notice me buying the thing, and so I didn't want to spend a lot of time reading packages and hovering around the Spanx display. Problem was, I didn't have my glasses with me, and some of the print was small. I looked through the packages of Spanx quickly and selected one that was for tall women and was the nude color I wanted.

When I got home, I stuffed it in a drawer and forgot about it until two weeks later when I was getting dressed for the wedding. I went upstairs, dreading how tough it would be to get the Spanx on. As I got the Spanx out of the package, I heard my 20-year-old son downstairs complaining about having to wear a tie. If he only knew how lucky he is, I thought.

The dress I was wearing was black and white, and most of the white was on the bottom. And even though I was 49, had gained weight and had occasional hot flashes like one does in menopause, I still had periods. Which is really, really not fair. If I had to suffer the bad menopause symptoms, couldn't I also have the good symptom? And these were not regular periods like I used to. have—not ones I could put on a calendar. They would just show up whenever they wanted to. Surprise! And when they arrived, they meant business, shall we say. I'd recently discovered that several of my good friends had all stopped their periods, and I was a bit jealous that I still had to go through it all. I was leery of wearing a white dress to a big event without fully protecting myself, which meant wearing a tampon and a pad. You ladies know the white clothing drill. I'd had enough embarrassing things happen to me in my life to know that if I didn't wear this double protection, then with my luck, something bad would surely happen when I was out in public.

So time was ticking by and it was almost time to leave for the wedding, and I was struggling—and I do mean struggling—to pull up my Spanx when all of a sudden I realized they were crotchless!! The hose material had an oval hole cut out right in the crotch. That's bad enough by itself because I wouldn't be comfortable in it and what is up with that anyway? Do they expect you to actually pee through that hole? But at that particular time my main concern was: where the hell do you stick a mini-pad if your under garment is crotchless? There was nothing about it on the package—at least not that I had seen when I bought it. Maybe it had been written in fine print somewhere, but I think something that important should be printed in huge letters. I sighed and looked at my watch, realizing I had to hurry. Then I heard my son complain again about how hard it was to tie a tie. He really, honestly had no clue! I felt like running down the stairs and wringing his neck, shouting, "My underwear doesn't have a crotch, and you are complaining about a tie?"

I ended up wearing the Spanx with another undergarment on top of it, which I think sort of defeats the purpose of the Spanx in the first place. In regard to any of these types of garments, let me officially say that I give up.

Martina McBride's hit song, "This is For the Girls," is wonderfully inspiring with advice for women at different ages of their lives: the struggles of peer pressure at 13, of chasing your dreams and saving pennies at 25, and of worrying about wrinkles at age 42. But then the song ends. As if that's it, life's done. Martina, I beg you, don't stop at 42—add at least one other verse to this song. Maybe about how terrific it is to be sixty and sexy and done with your periods. And done with those blasted crotchless undergarments.

Being Carded & Complimented

Most people getting older like to tell self-esteem-building stories of being carded when buying drinks, even though that doesn't necessarily mean they look under 21—the waitress is probably just being overly cautious. If the 'carding' isn't sincere, if the person honestly isn't sure if you are over 21 or not, then, hey, that's great. But I venture to say that in 99.5% of these 'older person carding' cases, the waitress or bartender doing the carding is totally sure the customer is over 21. They're just doing their jobs. Or maybe even trying to play with your mind a little bit.

When I was 53, I went to Target with Jason when he was almost 15 to buy the new Batman video game. The game is rated 'mature', so Jason gave me his money so I could purchase it since he was under 18. When I handed the money to the cashier—a guy who was probably in his early twenties—he said, "Could I see some ID please?"

I was confused because I thought he was asking my son for his ID. I told the cashier, "I'm the one buying it."

"Yes, I know," he replied. "But I need to see your ID."

I glanced at him and asked, "Seriously?"

"You have to be over 18 to buy it."

I narrowed my eyes at him, as if to tell him to stop playing with me or patronizing me or whatever he was doing. "Come on," I said.

"We have to make sure you are over 18."

Ok, I would have been flattered had it not been so outrageously obvious that I was definitely over 18. If I had to have been over 45 and he was carding me, then THAT would have been flattering because 45 was a hell of a lot more of a possibility that 18. Could he not see the wrinkles and age spots that are, I assume, quite rare in your average 18-year-old? I sighed and pulled out my license from my purse. He glanced at it and nodded. I know he was following the rules, but at some point, it does come off as just plain patronizing—like when nurses call me "Sweetie".

As we walked away, my son said, "Mom, you just got carded."

"I know," I replied bluntly, not amused. A smile tugged at the corners of his mouth.

Compliments have to come across as sincere if they are to be truly appreciated. My 93-year-old mother gives me some very sweet compliments about my looks sometimes, and I love her for that—but then I remember she has macular degeneration and needs a huge magnifying globe just to see pictures, and the lowest line she can see on the eye chart is the second one. Over the years, macular degeneration caused a blank, blurry spot in the center of her vision. But I guess I look okay, peripherally. Which is something at least.

At this stage of life—particularly for a woman—getting a sincere compliment really can make you feel good. The self-esteem can take a beating once you get past 45. At the mall one day, I ran into the mother of two guys that I grew up with whom I hadn't seen in a while.

So I asked her about them. "How are Dan and Mike?" I asked.

She replied, "Oh, just like you, getting older."

That is the last damn time I will ever ask that woman about her sons.

And having three sons and my husband around means that I rarely—possibly never—get true compliments once the boys passed the age of six.

So you will understand the significance of what happened to me in 2014 when I was in the grocery store. There I was getting some cilantro when I heard someone who was approaching me say, "Hey." I looked to my left to see a man in a blue Carolina Tar Heels sweatshirt. He then said something, but I wasn't sure what it was. It sounded a bit like 'cilantro' so he was probably asking me a question about it.

"Excuse me, what?" I asked. And then I heard music to my ears.

"You're not single are you?" he asked.

I was so surprised that I didn't know how to respond. So I just said, "No, no, I'm not."

The guy sighed and nodded his head. "I figured you weren't. Oh well." And then he was gone around the corner. Obviously, I am totally out of practice with this kind of thing. I hadn't had a compliment in ten years, much less what sounded like a pick-up line. I gave no witty comeback or anything to let the guy know I wasn't offended so he wouldn't be embarrassed. Nothing like, "Not in the last 25 years," said with an appreciative grin. I probably looked like a deer caught in the headlights. So disappointed in myself. I was not the same person who used to go out dancing with my friends in college and had no qualms about being approached or even doing the approaching. But still, it was a compliment. Kind of. In a way.

Another time when I was with my mom at the grocery store, a man came up to us and said to me, "I just wanted to tell you that you are gorgeous." Again, I was totally dumbfounded and didn't know what to say.

"Thank you, I mumbled, suddenly self-conscious.

My mother of course piped right up as mothers do. "That's what I always have told her, and she just won't believe it." The two of them stood there talking about my gorgeousness or lack thereof, while I stood awkwardly by holding a frozen pizza in my hands.

The moral of this story is: I obviously need to hang out in grocery stores more often.

From Miss to Ma'am

Up until a certain point in my life, the word 'ma'am' had always been reserved for women my mother's age and for teachers whatever their age. So it became obvious to me that time was indeed marching on when the "Miss" that I used to be addressed by was replaced by "Ma'am." I first noticed this switch when being greeted in retail stores. "May I help you, Miss?" sounds so much better than "May I help you, Ma'am?"

Another area I've noticed the 'Miss to Ma'am' thing is in law enforcement. When I was younger, I got stopped twice for some minor traffic violations and both times they called me "Miss." And both times I was let off with a warning. Then several years ago I got stopped for speeding on one of those short roads that go from 45 miles per hour to 35 mph to 25 mph very quickly. When the policeman came to the window, he asked, "How are you today, Ma'am?" And I knew I'd reached that point in life all women know must come. But it's still it's an unwelcome dose of reality.

Another police encounter occurred when I was driving back from Billy's high school. Jason and I had just picked Billy up after basketball practice; Billy wasn't feeling very well and reclined back in the seat. Jason was watching a Brady Bunch DVD, and I was listening to the episodes I knew by heart as I drove along. (Sometimes when I'm listening, I fantasize that I'm on *Who Wants to Be a Millionaire* and the million dollar question is something like "What was the name of Mr. Brady's boss on The Brady Bunch?" and I'd know it because of all the times I'd seen the show. By the way, his boss was Mr. Phillips.)

Anyway, as I made my way through all the traffic, I turned onto a road that was backed up as usual; it would probably take us ten minutes before we'd get around the curve and through the light. I needed to turn left, but I'd have to wait in the other lane that went straight until I got closer. Finally, I pulled out of the straight lane and into the left turn lane.

After I made my turn, there were blue lights and sirens behind me. "What did you do?" Billy asked.

"I have no earthly idea," I told him, easing the SUV over to the side of the road.

The officer came up to the window and said bluntly, "Did you know you were on the wrong side of the road?"

"What?" I said.

"What?" Billy repeated.

"You got over into the left turn lane too soon," the officer told me. "There was still a yellow line there."

"All I noticed was that there was a back-up in the straight lane and the left lane was almost empty," I replied. "I waited in the straight lane until I knew it was safe to get over."

"Well, you got over there too soon."

"Everybody else gets over at that same spot or even before," I told him, knowing it wasn't a good excuse, but it was true.

"I know they do, but we have to make an example out of somebody," he said.

An example???? That's me, all right, here to be made an example of. Yep, that's my mission in life.

"Umm," I began, "How am I an example when other people driving by still have no idea what I was stopped for? I mean, wouldn't it be better to post a sign that reminds people of the rule?"

He looked at me for a minute like perhaps I had a point. Then I remembered Billy. "And my son is not feeling well. He just finished basketball practice and I was trying to get him home."

He glanced at Billy, who bless his heart, gave the guy his best "I feel like I'm gonna throw up" face. "Tell ya what, Miss," the policeman said, "I'll just write you a warning ticket."

"Thank you, sir," I gushed, although I was still annoyed I'd been stopped in the first place. At least there would be no ticket, no higher insurance rates, no "Something happened coming home from Billy's school" conversations I'd have to have with Kevin. But as I drove off, the words that kept ringing in my ears were "Tell ya what, Miss"—the cop called me Miss! Getting off ticket-free was great too, but he called me Miss!

It's amazing the difference one little word can make in a person's life.

There was another time our family was Newark, New Jersey for a relative's anniversary celebration in 2009, and we had to take an airport train from one gate to another. Kevin, Jason, my niece, my mother-in-law, and I stepped into one of the train cars that already had a few men sitting in the only available seats. The only other option was to stand and hold on to the overhead bars, which was fine with me.

Just as we got on, I heard one of the men behind us say, "Ma'am, would you like to sit down?" I cringed. I was facing away from him and couldn't determine who exactly he was talking to, but the way my luck had been going lately in these situations, I feared he was talking to me. Now not only was I being called Ma'am, but I looked old enough for someone to offer me his seat! Crap. Leaning closer to Jason, I pulled him over to me, as if to say, "How the hell can you call me Ma'am when I'm the mom of an eight-year-old?"

Then I turned and looked at the man and saw that he was looking straight at my mother-in-law, not me. "Yes!" I exclaimed under my breath. I fist bumped Jason, and he looked at me strangely. The man got up, still looking at my mother-in-law and gestured toward his vacant seat. She thanked him and sat down. Whew! Embarrassing moment averted. I know sometime in the not-too-distant future I will become the older woman that nice men on trains give up their seats to, but I'm not ready to accept that role just yet. Going from "Miss" to "Ma'am" is simply one of life's transitions. But just remember, waiters—better tips await if you call me "Miss."

The Pursuit of Exercise

The older I get, the harder it is for me to get into an exercise routine. And yet, the older I get, the more I need it. Sure, I know there are those moms who always seem to find time to run a marathon while raising five kids and being CEO of some corporation. Sure, ever since pre-school there have been those size 2 moms who drop their kids off at school and go work out, coming back to pick up their kids after running five miles and doing Pilates, still looking gorgeous and radiant. Unfortunately, I'm not one of them. Going to the gym is just another item on my list of things to do. Before the kids came along, I used to go on a regular basis—okay, a semi-regular basis; but, during the years I spent at home raising them and making them my top priority, going to the Y took a back seat to their schedules. And now that my nest is almost empty, I find it hard to get motivated to get back in an exercise routine.

My gym card had gathered dust amidst the grocery store discount cards, insurance cards, and expired store coupons. When I do by some miracle happen to make it to the gym, it's been so long since I've been there that I have to re-read the posted instructions on those complicated exercise machines. I try to read them nonchalantly while stretching or checking my cell phone messages so everyone will think I know what I'm doing. Don't want to look out of shape *and* dumb. But all I can think about while I'm running or working on those machines is a list of things I have to do: pick up dry cleaning, make soup for a teacher luncheon, buy milk, finish a writing project, clean the bathrooms, fold laundry, and defrost the roast beef. It's an ever-revolving list; sometimes I even make up a little tune for it so I won't forget the items. I drove up to a Wendy's drive-thru one time and when they asked what I wanted to order, I told them, "notebook paper, cream of mushroom soup, and dish washing detergent." Obviously, I had my mind on my shopping list rather than the menu.

Working out is anything but stress-relieving for me like my husband says it is for him. If I had nothing else that I had to get done, then yes, I think working out would be okay. But I have to set some priorities. At the end of the day, no one is going to remember whether or not I've worked out, but they will know whether I bought milk or met a deadline on a writing project.

Kevin admonishes me sometimes for not working out on a regular basis, especially when each new year starts and it's time for resolutions. He's always after me to take better care of myself and not do stuff like staying up until 2 in the morning writing, eating Betty Crocker frosting straight from the can, or skipping my breakfast because morning was just too hectic. One year he asked me how my resolution was coming along. I'd made the resolution to take better care of my health.

"I took my vitamin this morning," I replied.

"What'd ya have for breakfast?" he asked. I didn't answer at first. Sort of like pleading the Fifth Amendment in a trial. "What'd ya have for breakfast?" Kevin repeated, wanting an answer.

I almost answered, "Whole wheat toast, fruit, and Metamucil." But I believe in honesty in a marriage so I came clean. "Two Excedrin and a cookie," I said. He gave me an exasperated look. "It was an oatmeal cookie," I added as if it would make a difference. He was not impressed.

I've honestly tried to make working out a routine. At one point when Billy was a toddler, I even selected a low-impact aerobics class and went to the first one with high hopes. But what in the world was that thing they called the 'grapevine' anyway? For those not familiar with this charming little number, the 'grapevine'—which is probably not even done in classes anymore—amounts to an aerobic line dance with lots of hopping on specific feet at specific times, making precise turns and twirls in sync with everybody else, all while making your way across the room and back. Something akin to the June Taylor dancers in sweats. I'm sorry, but I was looking for a little exercise, not the ultimate coordination challenge. I twirled left when everyone else went right, and I ended up tripping and falling down, my tall, big-boned body smack-dab in the middle of the floor. Memories of 7th grade gym class came flooding back.

The petite-while-buff-at-the-same-time aerobics instructor rushed over to me, asking in a sing-song cheerleader voice if I was okay (for the record, I did get up remarkably quick, looking very athletic as I bounded right up). Needless to say, I didn't go back to the aerobics class again. And now there are Pilates and Kickboxing and all kinds of stuff that just sounds like you have to be coordinated right from the start.

I've told Kevin many times over the years that housework and tending to the kids is actually exercise: picking up a forty pound pre-schooler and running through the parking lot in the rain, unloading heavy bags of groceries, scrubbing floors and bathrooms, opening tightly-closed jars of spaghetti sauce, sweeping, leaning over into the washer then down to the dryer, taking all the junk up and down stairs. Problem is it doesn't quite work on the right parts.

Honestly, there are reasons—legitimate reasons— that make it difficult for moms to exercise (follow me here). I call this the Pursuit of Exercise. For example: One time I recall, I decided to get back to an exercise routine. I'd neglected it for a while, mainly due to raising three boys, but also because I'd spent the past year writing and marketing a book. Sitting at the computer ten hours a day doesn't do a lot for one's figure. Well, it does do a lot, but it has the opposite effect of what you'd want it to have.

So anyway, I went up to Billy's room where we had an elliptical machine that allows you to run in place without putting the jarring stress on your legs and knees. It's kind of like running on two big skis in circles. Not that I've ever been on skis. Of course, I couldn't stand the thought of being bored while I ran, so I turned on my son's TV. But it didn't come on. I had to practically read the instruction booklet to figure out his video system. As I was in the midst of trying to figure out which switch to turn for what, I realized how awfully dusty his TV screen was. So I cleaned it.

Then I noticed that everywhere was pretty dusty, so I grabbed a tissue and started wiping down the furniture. Behind the TV, I saw 'stuff' back there. Stuff that needed to be picked up: empty Gatorade bottles, crumpled papers from old homework assignments, video game instruction booklets, etc. I moved the furniture around so I could get back there. When I moved his dresser, I saw some shirts sticking out of his drawer. I opened it, refolded the shirts, and put them back inside.

But that reminded me of the shirts I needed to take out of the dryer before they got wrinkled. I walked down the hall and did that. That's when I saw the pair of baseball cleats I'd bought for David that were too small for him. *"Where did I put that receipt?"* I thought to myself. The cleats had been on sale, and they wouldn't take them back without the receipt. I rushed downstairs to get my purse to see if I'd stuck the receipt in there, when I remembered I hadn't put the roast in the crock pot for that night's dinner. I put the roast in the pot with water and seasonings and set the timer (this was years before I hesitated using a crock pot due to a certain episode of *This is Us.*) After that, I looked through my purse, dug way to the bottom, and finally found the receipt.

As I started upstairs, I saw the dog sitting at the back door, meaning he needed to go out. I let him out and waited for him to do his duty, during which time I realized Jason had spilled Lucky Charms on the kitchen table and left his homework on the counter. I cleaned up the spill and let the dog in, making a mental note to drop my son's homework by the school later that day. I had an appointment at noon, so I'd take care of that then.

I went back up the stairs, started another load of laundry, and was just about to get back onto the elliptical when the phone rang. I answered that only to find it was someone calling for me to volunteer for something else. I mustered the strength to say 'no' although I almost caved under pressure. I finally climbed onto the elliptical thing, and was disappointed to find that I could only turn the TV to ESPN. I like ESPN, but in the middle of a week day, they don't have the most interesting of programming. I started running, and all those numbers on the handlebars flashed. I knew I could set the equipment for certain levels, but I had no idea how to and didn't have the time to figure it out. I assumed it started on the lowest level, so I just started running before I lost my incentive to do so.

After a minute, I stopped, exhausted, practically lying all over the handlebars. I knew I was out of shape, but this was ridiculous. I'd been to the gym in the past couple of months and I could run around the track without feeling like this. I was able to run ten minutes, but I had to stop every minute and lean over the handlebars, gasping for air. When I finally got off of this contraption, my legs felt like they were made of concrete. My heart was just about pounding out of my chest, and I silently recited the warning signs of a heart attack.

I made it down the stairs, got a bottle of water, and plopped down on the couch. Whew! I rested up for a few minutes before I had to go take a shower to get ready for my noon meeting. Later that day, I asked Billy if the elliptical starts out on the easiest level. He told me, no, that it starts at whatever it was on previously. He smiled and said, "I bet you had the incline setting on high. It goes from 1-10 with 10 being the highest." He went up and checked and yelled down, "Mom, you had it on level 6."

"Thank you, Jesus!" I shouted, relieved that I wasn't quite as out of shape as I'd thought. Maybe there is still some hope that I can finally get into an exercise routine. Better late than never. Still, trying to 'work out' is difficult for moms because, as this case demonstrates, often one thing leads to another and then to another, making it almost impossible to devote a mom's attention to the pursuit of exercise. But an older mom realizes all too well that with metabolism and hormone changes, she could get away with not exercising a lot easier when she was younger. I've been trying to go to the Y to walk and run on the track and lift weights, but my visits are sporadic. Everyone checking into the Y slides their membership card through the machine at the entrance. But I have to say I really don't like that the people behind the front desk can see on the computer screen how long it's been since my last visit. "Welcome back, Sharon!" they say cheerfully as if I'd been stranded on a deserted island somewhere for years and had finally returned home.

Come on y'all, it hasn't been *that* long.

The Back Surgery

Back surgery is usually thought of as something older adults undergo, due to the aging process and the wear and tear on their backs. So it was difficult and rather humbling for me when I began to have severe back pain in the summer of '08 at the age of 46 and realized that back surgery might be the only answer. I wanted to yell, "But this can't be happening—I've got a kid in elementary school!" How many moms of second graders have to go in for back surgery?

The pain started in a spot in my left shoulder blade one day in mid-July, and I put a moist heating pad on it, thinking it was a muscle strain. I was in the midst of finishing the rough draft for a book plus several more writing projects, and so I attributed the pain to too much time on the computer. After a few days, the pain began to travel across my shoulder and into my left arm, making my arm ache all the way down to my wrist.

A few days later, I had an MRI which showed a large herniated area between disc 6 and disc 7 of the cervical spine and that it was pinching a nerve that lead to my left arm. During a consultation with a neurosurgeon, he noticed the weakness that I had in my left arm, in addition to the pain. His concern was that steroids might help the pain, but they would not help the weakness and that the nerve damage could actually become worse. He also said that in a situation involving weakness, surgery was almost always done for the best outcome.

Okay, I thought. Back surgery. I could handle that. It wouldn't be pleasant, but it would alleviate the pain I was feeling and I would stay in the hospital overnight, the thought of which was exciting. It's pretty sad when moms look at a night in the hospital as a mini-vacation.

Then the doctor explained that since the disc was in the upper back—the cervical spine region—that they would "go in through the neck." I reached around under my hair and felt the back of my neck. He paused and then added as gently as he could, "the front of the neck."

Whoa, whoa, whoa. We were talking *back* surgery here, right?? As in back of the body, not the front of the body. So what was this cutting the front of the neck thing? I was beginning to feel very Jack the Ripperish. Surely I must have misunderstood something. So I asked for him to repeat that part again, trying not to appear too panicky: "What was the reason again for going through the front of the neck for back surgery?" I asked, hoping the doctor would say, "Oh that's right, you're here for the *back* surgery; I was confusing you with the woman in the next room who has to have an invasive tonsillectomy." Or something. But nope, there had been no mistake. The doctor explained that since my herniated disc was high in my shoulder blade area that it would be easier to go in through the front of the neck instead of through the bone and muscle in the back. I decided not to ask exactly *how* he would get to my back once he was inside my neck; this was one of those times ignorance was indeed bliss. He did say that the scar would be minimal and usually the incision is done in a fold in the neck. He looked at me and said, "You don't really have any folds in the neck,"—which made me almost want to hug the man—"but we'll find a good place for it." He went on to explain that two screws would be placed between the discs and eventually it'd all fuse together.

As I drove away from his office, the bad news was that I'd have to have back surgery, but the good news was he said I didn't have any folds in my neck (though to be fair he didn't see me with my neck bent over). When you get to be a certain age, off-hand compliments in the course of conversations about other things tend to take center stage.

The surgery itself went well, even though my neck was bandaged, and it was hard to swallow. I remember nothing about it except waking up and getting some pain meds through an IV. However, the only room in the hospital available for me was a room with a sliding glass door that ran the width of the room instead of a heavy wooden one that kept out hallway lights and noise. This meant more noise and light into the room—or rather 'area'—as I came to call my space. I felt like I'd been put out on the patio. The room also had a toilet that pulled out from under the sink, rather than a complete separately enclosed bathroom as other rooms had, a particularly endearing feature when a nurse or visitors were in the room with me when I had to go.

Kevin and the boys came to see me around dinner time, and I think they were a little shocked by the huge, blood-stained bandage on my neck. The visit was short since they had to get David to a basketball game, but none of the guys got in a fight while they were there and no one was asked to leave for being too loud, so the visit was a success. My parents came to visit too, and I thought how ironic it was that my 80-something year old parents were coming to see ME in the hospital after back surgery instead of the other way around. Our family really was blessed to have them both be so healthy.

My meals consisted of pudding and chicken broth since it was hard to swallow. I felt like I was practicing for the old folks' home. When the nurse brought in pain pills to swallow, I looked at the oblong pills dubiously. "No way," I managed to whisper. This is when I was told that bending your neck forward when you swallow pills actually closes off the windpipe, making it much easier to swallow than does leaning your head back like most people do. I only wish someone had told me this when I had to swallow those horse-sized pre-natal vitamins during pregnancy.

I tried to pass the time by watching some TV. Once I surfed past a baseball game to another channel, but then I flipped immediately back to the game because I realized the little diagram at the top of the screen with three yellow dots on the baseball diamond meant the bases were loaded. As a mom of boys, I could fully appreciate the intensity and drama of the situation. Would the pitcher get out of this jam? As a writer, I've always sort of admired how that little diamond-shaped diagram in the corner of the screen can summarize the whole story of the game: what inning it is, what team is at bat, how many outs, how many strikes and balls, how many on base, and of course, the score. Just at that moment, a nurse came in and saw me watching baseball. She huffed, "Baseball on TV—that would certainly make me go to sleep." Obviously not a mom of boys.

"Bases are loaded," I told her, but she didn't seem to care.

Kevin, my mother, and my sisters all offered to spend the night with me at the hospital, but I told them I'd be fine and there was no need for them to stay. I was looking forward to a little time alone. I'd even brought a book along to read. I'd spent the night in the hospital before when my mother was a patient, and she had a pretty restful time there. As the night progressed, I started feeling worse, though, and I realized my time there would not be restful. I turned off the TV around 9:00 because my head started pounding, making me feel nauseated. The light and noise from the hallway made it worse. Sometimes when the nurses came in to check my vital signs, they forgot to close the sliding glass door when they left, which increased the noise and light. That, plus lack of food and sleep, and oh yeah—*surgery*—combined to give me a heck of a migraine headache that persisted throughout the night. They came to get me at 6:30 for an x-ray, and I'd only had about an hour's sleep all night. I felt better after getting out of that terrible room, and I was soon getting ready to leave the hospital.

When I finally got home, my bed—even with the piles of laundry surrounding it—was the most wonderful place on earth. I still I had some trouble swallowing and eating, but that improved with time. Friends and family offered to help out with meals since I wouldn't feel like cooking for the guys, but I told them all not to worry about it. As I said to a friend from church when she asked about people bringing over meals, "My guys are actually okay with just opening a can of Beefaronii." I felt bad that they wanted to bring home-cooked meals for the guys, like they were stepping in for me in what they thought was our normal routine, when I rarely did homemade, from scratch cooking.

When the bandage came off a few weeks later, yes, there was a scar on my neck, but that, too, would get better. Of course, there were more creams and ointments I had to use to minimize the scar. I did find, however, that worrying about the scar distracted me from worrying about my wrinkles.

The operation was successful though, and I was grateful to be free of the excruciating pain that I had felt in my left arm. I still had muscle spasms in my shoulders occasionally, and this provided a pretty good excuse for telling the guys that I couldn't pull the clothes out of the washer or scrub the bathroom shower like I used to be able to do.

Soon after the surgery, I was mentioning to someone about how I had to have back surgery and I was only 47. Kevin, who was with me, eyed me quizzically.

"You're 46," he said.

I paused for a moment and then smiled, realizing he was right. "I *am* only 46!" I squealed. The whole damn year for some reason, I'd been thinking I was already 47. I had just gained another whole year; it was like a last minute reprieve from the governor.

For several months after the surgery, I had to go for some follow-up x-rays to make sure everything was healing properly. I have to admit that I looked forward to these visits to the back surgeon because every time I was there I was always the youngest patient in the waiting room. The room was always crowded, and there I'd sit amongst the little ladies with walkers and old men with canes, and my still-ovulating-self would get a quick burst of self-esteem. The office was like a veritable fountain of youth for me.

At least, it was until that thirty-something hussy nurse strutted into the room. Damn.

My Grand Exit

"Have you fallen in the past six months?" Once you get a certain age, this is a standard question that doctors ask you at physicals. The first time they ask it, you realize you are officially over the hill. Of course, you reply adamantly, "No, I don't have any problems with falling." You want to retain your pride.

But the first time I was asked that at the age of 50, I had to say yes.

So it was like this: I decided for my son David's high school graduation recognition at our church the Sunday before the graduation ceremony that I would actually wear a dress instead of my usual pants. Got new shoes too—with heels, not flats. As I was walking down the carpeted steps that are the main exit out of the church, I was talking with Susan, a friend I hadn't seen recently. The line was moving slowly as people stopped at the bottom of the steps to speak with the minister. My church is very large with several ministers, and it is a Methodist church in which the ministers stay at a church for a while and then move on to another church; I had known other ministers very well but so far, I had not officially met the head minister who was talking to people at the bottom of the steps.

I turned away from Susan to speak to the minister, thinking I'd already gone down all the steps. Wrong. Had one more to go. Fell down right in front of everybody, igniting gasps. I remember looking up at the ceiling above me and thinking that it was a dream. But it wasn't. The minister helped me up, and I was okay but couldn't believe that had happened. Susan did say that I fell "gracefully". I think she was just being nice because David and Jason were several people behind me, and they did not use the word 'graceful' in their description of the event. Eleven-year-old Jason said, "Mom, I realized someone fell and thought it was some old lady, and then I realized it was you."

David said he was impressed with how I '"ducked under the railing" so I didn't hit my head, and I told him that there was no ducking involved because I had no control over my body at that point. No time to think about sliding or ducking. It was quite the scene in the vestibule that day. My grand exit.

About six months later when I was volunteering in Jason's confirmation class, I saw the minister from that day sitting alone at a nearby table. He looked up and nodded at me. I figured that I would go ahead and introduce myself since I was there and wanted to be polite.

"Hi, Reverend," I said. "I don't know if you remember me or not, but I'm the one who fell down the steps at the graduation service in the spring."

"Oh, I remember you!" he said, smiling at me.

Okay, I'd really rather that he would have paused a moment as he seemed to be thinking, searching his mind to recall where he had met me before, and then said something like, "Ahhh, yes, that's right. I do remember that now."

But nope, it was an immediate response that let me know I had left an indelible impression on him. I was not about to ask exactly what it was he remembered.

Childhood Déjà Vu

I've always hated roller skating. Well, not exactly roller skating itself, but I hated *trying* to roller skate when I was growing up. Big difference between trying and actually doing. We each have those memories from childhood about things we really dreaded because we weren't good at them and knew we'd probably embarrass ourselves. There's the proverbial being picked last for a team in P.E. or being called on to answer a question in math when we have no earthly idea what the teacher's talking about. Once we entered adulthood, we breathed a sigh of relief that we could leave behind such things and never have to do them again. Ever.

Then one day when you least expect it, that thing you dreaded in childhood comes back into your life. Like the time I ran into my tenth grade geometry teacher at a business event with my husband, how I prayed that she wouldn't remember me or that time I tried in vain to explain a homework problem on the board. Embarrassing moments tucked away in some cob-webbed corner of our minds can suddenly come alive again. An unwelcome sense of déjà vu.

As a child, I detested trying to roller skate due to its high embarrassment potential. I'm not the most coordinated person even when I'm not on wheels, so putting me on skates is like taking the Bad News Bears and blindfolding them. Back then learning to skate was done by the trial and error method *in front of everyone* instead of in skating classes. Over the years, I've found if I have to do something remotely athletic in front of others, I become a complete klutz. The bottom line is nobody wants to look stupid when somebody's watching.

Growing up, I'd occasionally go to the rink with my church youth group. Once there, I'd run into acquaintances from school and become self-conscious about my awkward skating. I had to grip the railing or my feet would fly out from under me, leaving me collapsed in a heap. Yet, the most humiliating part was trying to get up again because each time I tried to stand up, my foot would roll out from under me. It would have been easier just to crawl off the rink, but my pride wouldn't let me. Once I got to the side of the rink, I watched the skaters glide by me and ached a bit inside because it looked like such fun.

As a teenager, I had to face my phobia again. I don't know why I agreed to go to a roller skating rink on a first date. Momentary insanity? Desperation for a date? I just wanted to go somewhere with a cute guy, and this cute guy had asked me to go skating. Too bad it couldn't have been to a movie or even the bargain pizza buffet. If I asked for a change of venue, I was afraid he'd just withdraw the offer altogether. Yet, the thought of trying to look good on skates while partaking in clever first-date conversation made me slightly nauseated.

I panicked so much at the prospect of making a fool out of myself in front of Mr. Wonderful that I had my two older sisters take me skating the night before so they could teach me. My concern was that Mr. Wonderful was anticipating a fun night of us holding hands as we zoomed around the rink together, in perfect, coordinated, graceful unison. Graceful, I was not. One of my sisters told me not to "flap" my arms when I was falling backward. Believe me sis, I wasn't flapping them on purpose; it was purely instinctive. Doing an impression of a crow in flight was not exactly the pose I wanted to strike for my new boyfriend.

Despite my sisters' best efforts, they didn't impart a lot of skating know-how to me, and I seriously thought about telling Mr. Wonderful that I'd sprained my ankle. Wrap it up and limp a little and he'd never know the difference. Alas, I decided not to lie and went through with the skating date, though I fell many times. Yes, it was embarrassing, but he would help me up, giving us an excuse to get close. He actually said I was cute when I fell, obviously reveling in his rescuer role. I never knew that being a klutz was cute. During the romantic couples skate, the lights dimmed and the music slowed, as he put his arms around me to hold me up. As the Bee Gees crooned, "How Deep is Your Love," I even managed to lean my head on Mr. Wonderful's chest a few times. Still, I was relieved when the night was over, knowing I'd never have to deal with skating again.

Fast forward nineteen years to 1998. David and Billy, then ages 3 and 6, and I were watching a *Full House* rerun, a pastime made rather enjoyable for moms due to the frequent on-screen presence of Uncle Jesse, aka John Stamos with dark good looks and gorgeous hair. (Have mercy!) Then Kevin came in the door with the mail, tossing the innocent-looking birthday party invitation for Billy on the counter. "Yippee!" Billy shouted. "It's at a skating rink!" All the color drained from my face as I realized my childhood fear was back.

I grabbed the invitation to check the date, hoping we'd be out of town that weekend and have a legitimate excuse. No such luck. Billy really wanted to go to the party, and so I relented—against my better judgment. He didn't know how to skate, and I didn't want him frantically grasping the railing at the party. Or flapping his arms.

And the big question was: would parents be expected to skate too? I figured if their own kids couldn't skate, there was probably an unwritten rule that the parents had to get out there and help them. Thank God there was enough time to get Billy some help, so I signed him up for skating lessons a few weeks before the party. That first day, I was anxious for him as he stepped onto the rink. My hands were sweaty, and there was a lump in my throat. I remembered these painfully familiar feelings all too well. Surprisingly, my son was pretty good on skates, and I wondered for a second if he'd been switched at birth with another baby.

The adult classes were going on simultaneously on the other end of the rink. Two women I knew had taken these classes previously and both broke a wrist. All the more reason for me never to try it. I greatly admired the four adults out there—one man and three women— taking baby steps on skates and repeatedly falling on their butts onto the hard floor. An instructor must have noticed my forlorn gaze toward the rink. "Why don't you try it?" she asked.

"Oh, I don't think so," I replied.

She smiled. "There's another class Friday."

"Skating has never been my thing," I explained, shaking my head.

The woman was undaunted. "Tell ya what," she persisted, " I'll let you have the first lesson free. And if you sign up today, you'll can get half off on a new pair of skates and a coupon for a free pizza at the snack stand." I was apparently talking to a skating instructor who had once sold time share vacations for a living. "As tempting as that is," I told her, "I'll have to pass." I smiled and turned to watch my son, who was gradually improving and certainly not going to follow in his mom's footsteps when it came to roller skating.

Looking back on my early days at the rink, I realize nobody probably even noticed my clumsiness. Sometimes I wish I could go back and learn to skate without being insecure. Memories about things we dreaded when we were young have a way of popping back into our lives—sometimes through our own adult experiences and sometimes through our children. Some people decide to conquer their fears the second or even third time around, while others—like me—choose to live with them, while realizing they might resurface to haunt us.

So I'll probably never get on skates again.[2] You don't look nearly as cute being a klutz at age 50 as you do at 16.

---

2   (Unless it's for a couples skate with John Stamos.)

Mrs. Allison

As I get older, I often look back and fondly remember the people who helped me become the person I am. Since the title of this book includes the PTA, I would be remiss if I didn't pay tribute to one of my teachers who meant so much to me and was such an inspiration.

In January of 2003, I was relaxing on my couch one morning, perusing a copy of Raleigh's newspaper, *The News & Observer*, casually scanning the news. When I turned to the obituary page, I saw her picture immediately—right at the very top of the far left column; I couldn't miss it. I quickly sat up straight, my hands clutching the paper. The photo was from a time in her life before I had known her, maybe thirty years before I first stepped into her classroom. But her face was unmistakable—her kind eyes, her familiar smile.

The obituary gave her age as 77, which was about what I thought she'd be by then, though I'll always imagine her the way she was in 1980 when she was my English teacher at Raleigh's Athens Drive High. The paper also said she died after an extended illness, and I felt terrible that I hadn't known she'd been sick. Disbelief set in. My eyes darted above the picture to double-check the name. There it was again: *Muriel Waters Allison*.

The newspaper collapsed in my hands, and my tears came suddenly and unexpectedly, emptiness welling up within me. It hurt to know I would never hear her voice again, never be encouraged by her optimism or inspired by her impassioned ranting and raving. During my junior and senior years from 1978-1980, I was in Mrs. Allison's English class at Athens Drive, but I'd kept in touch with her many years after that.

I'd never had a teacher quite like her before. I could hear in her voice how genuinely excited she was about teaching. Suddenly English wasn't just grammar and literary terms. That English class stirred something inside of me that I hadn't known existed. In her class, I discovered I was a sensitive person and could actually express emotions that most people could only feel. It felt good when I began to see that I could touch my parents and my friends with my writing.

The reason I began to feel things so deeply was because I could see that Mrs. Allison felt things deeply, too, and **she wasn't afraid to show it**. I didn't feel as vulnerable anymore because I knew she understood me, that it was okay and even good to express emotions and thoughts in words. Her enthusiasm was contagious. I always looked forward to sitting at my desk listening to one of Mrs. Allison's lectures about Antigone or "Death of a Salesman"—lectures she managed to turn into lessons about life, lectures filled with her boundless wisdom and humor.

Sometimes my classmates and I would come into the room, ready to take notes about Joseph Conrad or metaphors and then we'd quickly realize there'd been a change in plans: Mrs. Allison wanted to talk about a current event or a past experience that was on her mind, and she'd get on a roll, almost as if she were on stage doing a monologue. Sometimes she'd walk out of her class and across the hall to the supply room to get a book or another item, continuing her impromptu lecture all the while. Then she'd step back into the room, never missing a beat. As she went on with her 'lesson about life lecture,' my classmates and I would glance at each other and smile, maybe shake our heads in awe, knowing how blessed we were to be sitting in a Muriel Allison classroom.

There were many times something she would say would move me so much I would grab my pencil and start scribbling my feelings down in my English notebook. Class notes often had some of my own poetry written around the edges of the paper. It felt wonderful to capture something I was feeling at the moment and put it in writing. I'd felt like that before but not to the extent Mrs. Allison made me feel it.

One time during the first weeks of my junior year, Mrs. Allison put all other class activities on hold until someone in the class came up with a thesis sentence for an analysis paper we were all writing. She said eventually someone would write a creative thesis sentence that would knock her socks off; but, until someone came up with it, nobody could write any further. In the quiet of the room students would walk over to her and show her their sentences. Mrs. Allison would read it and then shake her head "no". "That's good, but that just isn't 'it' yet," she said.

I'll never forget my own slow walk up to her desk. I showed her my thesis sentence and prepared myself for constructive criticism. She read the sentence, let out a war whoop, grabbed the paper out of my hand, and literally danced across the room, waving the paper in the air like a flag. "This is it!" she yelled. "This is it!" I had never known that "it" was somewhere inside of me waiting to get out. With Mrs. Allison, I felt confident enough to take down my walls and let "it" out. When I sometimes received a graded paper back from her with the words "See Me" scrawled across the bottom above her initials, "MWA", I'd feel nauseated briefly because she could be intimidating; but, I knew her suggestions to improve my work would only help me to become a better writer.

There was another time that stands out in my mind when Athens, a new high school at that time, had to be officially accredited. A committee of VIPs visited our school to sit in on some classes and to talk with students and teachers to see if Athens was worthy of accreditation. The day before the committee's visit, I had to give a presentation in Mrs. Allison's class—an oral poetry analysis of a Wordsworth poem— something about a daffodil, if I remember correctly. I gave a 25 minute speech, aware that Mrs. Allison liked my presentation because she was nodding her head in approval as I spoke. When I sat down, she told the class that the accreditation committee would be visiting our class the next day. Then she turned to me and announced, "Girl, you're going to get up there and give that analysis again and act like it's the first time you ever gave it." She turned to the rest of the class. "And everybody else is going to sit here and listen and act like they never heard it before." So the next day, we re-enacted it, and though I was nervous, things went well.

Muriel W. Allison taught English for a phenomenal 56 years—phenomenal not just because of the quantity but because of the quality. She was one of the first African-American teachers in Wake County's desegregated schools, having to prove herself to a lot of doubters at Broughton High. Initially, many parents didn't want their children to be in her classroom, but by halfway through the first semester, those same parents were standing in line, clamoring to have their kids placed in her class.

Prove herself she did, as she always earned a stellar reputation and teaching record wherever she taught, with her students routinely winning writing contests and scholarships. She had found 'it' hiding somewhere in other students, too. In April of 1982, she was named Tar Heel of the Week by *The News & Observer*. She also won a state humanities award and was featured on a WTVD-TV public affairs show.

When my classmates and I were applying to colleges in the fall of our senior year, Mrs. Allison helped each of us craft a personal essay to submit with our application; this was before essays were required as part of the submission. My essay was entitled, "To Grow in Spring," comparing growing up and leaving the nest to springtime, which Mrs. Allison went absolutely nuts over, particularly a phrase I used I still remember today: 'the nectar of my soul'. I still believe this essay is the reason I was admitted to UNC-Chapel Hill (despite my math grades) where I later received my degree in journalism.

At the end of my senior year, our English class went to a dinner theater to see the play "Camelot" because we had studied King Arthur and his round table, where no one person is at the head but all are equal and all are honorable. Mrs. Allison was sitting at the table beside mine. The play was fantastic: the acting, the music, the direction, the passion. The beautiful concept of Camelot came to life right before our eyes. In one of the final scenes of the play, King Arthur tells a young boy to never let Camelot die. He tells the young boy to say it loud, and the little boy shouts, "Camelot!" Then King Arthur passes 'Camelot' to him, in hopes that the boy will keep it alive. "Run boy, run!" Arthur tells him. "Run and tell the story of Camelot and then all the generations after you will know that once there was a place called Camelot." The scene is a spine-tingling, soul-bursting one for me.

As the boy was yelling "Camelot!" and running off stage, I looked over at Mrs. Allison. She was sitting there with tears streaming down her face with the palm of one hand pressed against her forehead. She kept shaking her head in disbelief and fidgeting in her chair. She couldn't sit still. I felt the same way. That scene inspired me so much that I wanted to jump up and somehow make everyone in the world experience the same emotion I felt. I wanted to share it with the world and then surely there would be no more wars. I knew exactly what Mrs. Allison was feeling. I looked again at the tears on her cheeks and her hand clinching a tissue, wiping her eyes. That May night in the dinner theater was the time I was proudest to call her my teacher. She wasn't afraid to show her students how moved she was, to show us how touching art can be.

Mrs. Allison signed my senior high yearbook by using a famous quote from poet Robert Browning: "Ah, but a man's reach should exceed his grasp—or what's a Heaven for." This quote was definitely food for thought for me, an 18-year-old setting off on college adventures. I suppose people interpret the quote in different ways, but to me then and to me now, it means this: while a person is on earth, he should always strive, should always keep reaching, will always be yearning—and all that reaching is good for us and makes us better people. We strive to do something and we do it—or grasp it—and then we reach even higher. But our yearning will never really be fulfilled on earth; that's what heaven is for. Yet, you need to keep reaching and not giving up here on earth for it to mean anything. I've thought about that quote so many times over the years.

During college, sometimes when I'd come home for the weekend, I'd stop by Athens on a Friday after school to chat with Mrs. Allison, knowing she'd understand my feelings, knowing I'd come away refreshed and motivated. She never failed me. Sometimes we'd talk for an hour or two, sitting there in her empty classroom when she could have already left for the day. College was, at first, very disillusioning to me, and I needed a 'dose' of Mrs. Allison's wisdom to get by.

I remember well the time she told me that when a person goes to college he must have both feet planted firmly on the ground. "If one foot is on a banana peel," she said, "then the person will slip and fall. And I don't want to even talk about having both feet on a banana peel." I saw her words firsthand as so many people in college cared more about getting drunk than achieving their dreams or retaining their integrity or identity. I often silently wished that those students could spend ten minutes in a Muriel Allison classroom because it would change their perspective on life.

As happens over time, I lost touch with Mrs. Allison, about the same time I started raising a family. We had sent each other Christmas cards for over a decade, but for some reason stopped. My last correspondence from her was in 1992 when she'd sent a note to say the photo I'd sent of my toddler was "beautiful!" I hadn't been aware of her having any severe health problems. I thought she was still living in her home in a nearby suburb, enjoying her golden years, reading poetry, maybe going to a play every now and then that would touch her soul. "Call Mrs. Allison" was on my perpetual to-do list.

Then came her obituary in the newspaper. I'd never known she had an extended illness, and I hope she knows I hadn't forgotten her. Many years earlier, I had sent her a note that included some of these memories of her and what they'd meant to me, and I was glad I'd sent it. Still, I wish I'd had the chance to tell her one more time how I felt about her. I'm glad Mrs. Allison found the elusive 'it' inside of me. She made me realize that as long as I'm living, I can't settle for less than what I can dream. Along the way, maybe I can pass 'it' along to someone else, just as King Arthur passed Camelot to the boy and Mrs. Allison passed 'it' to me. I ache knowing she is no longer on this earth.

When I sent flowers to her funeral, I paused, struggling to decide what I could write on the small accompanying card. What few words could possibly describe the depth of my feelings about this person? How could I say good-bye to her? And then it came to me, and I wrote: "Ah but a man's reach should exceed his grasp or what's a Heaven for."

V
Forever Young

The heart has no wrinkles.

—Marie de Sevigne

Chasing Dreams

When I was 41, I heard a guest on one of the morning news shows say that women over 40 need to accept their life as it is because chances are it won't change any by the time they've reached that age. The person even went so far as to say women at that age had probably already achieved all that they would in their lives. I heard that and thought, *"I don't think so."* I was indeed happy with my life, but I didn't feel that meant I wouldn't accomplish anything else or decide to take any new directions. Being an older mom also meant I still had a preschooler around the house, so it made it even more difficult to pursue new directions. But it was possible, and I wanted to do it.

I'd been writing a family life column for our town newspaper for the past five years and had even picked up an award or two for the column. I was also teaching writing classes through the local arts council and doing some public relations consulting and lots of volunteer work. And of course, my husband and I had three sons who kept us busy. My life was definitely full, but I wasn't about to accept that that's all there would be to my life. Perhaps, I thought, it was time to put the pursuit of my dreams into a higher gear.

Ever since my college days, I had tried to get a novel and a children's story published, but despite some 'almosts', the dream of having a book published still eluded me. In my 20s and 30s, I went after this dream tirelessly, but to no avail. This included an article published in *Good Housekeeping*; third place in a short story contest at a national writer's conference; a short story publication in the Raleigh newspaper; two revisions with a major publisher on a children's story before they turned it down; a New York literary agent who loved my completed novel and fought three months to have her agency represent it, only to be vetoed by her boss; a producer acquaintance of mine in Hollywood who thought a TV script I wrote was good enough to send to his agent, but the agent didn't think it was quite strong enough; and being named a semi-finalist in a national contest for a novel-in-progress.

I started wondering when someone knows it's time to give up on a dream, to get back to normal life and enjoy it without always being in steady pursuit of something seemingly out of reach. Going after a dream can indeed give meaning to life, but it can also be extremely frustrating. There had been many times I was ready to give up, but I couldn't because dreams are simply hard to let go, even if it means years of late nights spent at the computer or thousands of dollars in writers' conference fees and classes. Dreams require sacrifice. I'd been mulling over the possibility of trying to get some of my essays published in a book. *Someday*, I'd think.

When I heard the comments on the talk show about older women probably not achieving any more goals in their lives, I felt more motivated than ever and that's when I took my dream for someday and tried to turn it into a reality. Soon after this epiphany of sorts, I found an agent who agreed to pitch my latest book idea, which was a collection of humor essays about living in a household where I was the only female with my husband, three sons, and male dog. The big New York publishers that looked at the sample chapters said they liked the writing—some even loved it—but they turned the project down because I wasn't well-known. It seems that nowadays a person has to do something bad or strange in order to get a book contract. The quality of the writing doesn't even seem to matter, only if the writer or topic is in the news. I even started to think of weird things I could do to get instant fame and a book contract. Climbing the Empire State building in a Superwoman cape was not an option. Neither was faking my own kidnapping and rescue. At the time, it seemed that having an affair with a politician was the best way to get a book contract, but I really didn't want to go that far. I'd have to just keep on trying the traditional way to get published. But you see how the frustration of being a writer in this fame-crazy society makes a person start contemplating lame-brain ways to get a book publisher.

Most of the rejection letters I'd received were very complimentary, but a rejection is still a rejection. I intended to save all the rejection letters so that one day when I was published, I could inspire other writers with the volume of those early rejections; but, I ended up throwing away a lot of those because I simply needed the closet space. I was rapidly losing the optimism I'd had for twenty years, the belief that one day I'd have a book published. I'd spent thousands of dollars pursuing this dream—postage and copying costs along with a trip to LA to pitch a screenplay I'd written—and not to mention the time and neglect of other duties. Sometimes I'd feel guilty writing on my computer, when I really should have taken my kids to the park instead. And all I had to show for all my work was a file cabinet full of 'almosts.' There were times I'd think—okay, that's it—no more—only I'd have another idea come to me that I just had to put on paper or I'd read about another agent I felt compelled to contact. My dream would not leave me alone.

Finally, in November of 2005, it happened: my agent got a call from a publisher in Tennessee and they were interested in "House of Testosterone." I will never forget that autumn day when an email from my agent popped up in my in-box. I braced myself for more rejection and started to read it. To my surprise, it was an offer from a publisher to publish my book. To make sure my eyes weren't deceiving me, I called out to Billy, who was then 14. "Come look at this!" I shouted.

Billy came and read over my shoulder and then exclaimed, "Are you kidding me?" And that was the way it started. Sometimes dreams can become burdens when a person wants to reach a goal so badly only to keep getting disappointed. With this book contract, I felt like a weight was lifted from my shoulders.

The book was released in hard cover in December of 2006, had okay sales for a small publisher, and was named a notable book selection by Book Sense, a nation-wide group of independent book stores. Then a major publisher, Houghton Mifflin, contacted the small publisher and expressed an interest in buying the paperback rights to the book.

In April of 2007, the small publisher editor told me that he was expecting a call from Houghton Mifflin in the next few days to discuss paperback rights. He wanted me to do a conference call with the two of them, but he wasn't sure when the call would come. He told me he'd try to call me a few hours before the call to let me know. The problem was that my family and I were on vacation in Florida, and so I'd probably have to take the call on my cell phone and not be sure of the reliability of the coverage in the area. I carried my phone with me at all time for the next two days.

On the third day, we spent the morning at Busch Gardens in Tampa. We were standing in line for a ride, when I noticed that my cell phone was saying I had a message. I hadn't heard it ring at all. The message was from the small publisher who said he and the Houghton Mifflin publisher would be calling me at 1:00. It was then 12:30. I didn't want to have such an important conversation in the middle of an amusement park where I couldn't hear well, the coverage was spotty, and my kids were around. All my notes that I wanted to go over were also back in the car. That's when I started my race back to the parking lot. I ran through the park, dodging candy cotton vendors, wiping sweat from my brow. Finally, I reached the car at 12:51, turned on the air conditioning, looked over my notes, and got ready for the call. There was a Red Sox game on TV that afternoon—the opening game of the season—and my guys wanted to get back to the camper to watch. Thus, I knew they would soon be returning to the car. I'd told Kevin not to let them near the car if he could see I was still on the phone.

The phone call went well, but it took longer than expected. At one point, I looked up to see my three sons coming toward the car. David and Jason were running out in front, obviously racing to see who would get to the car first. I could hear them shouting and teasing already. As I watched them, I held up one hand to signal them to stop and shook my head wildly back and forth. I mouthed the word, "No!" silently. The whole thing seemed to be in slow motion like on those carpet cleaner commercials where the glass of red wine is about to fall on the white carpet and the mom is running toward it to catch it right in the nick of time. Only she didn't have to worry about impressing a publisher. Kevin was nowhere to be seen; I'd have to make eye contact with Billy, who was running now, too. I met his eyes and shook my head again and pointed to the phone. He got the message and held back the other two boys so they couldn't get in the car. Then Kevin came up from behind, and Billy filled him in about the situation. A few minutes later my phone conversation was over, and I let the boys into the car. I couldn't believe I was able to calmly carry on the phone conversations they were rushing toward the car—a possible disaster in the making.

The paperback book deal was eventually done, and it was released near Mother's Day of 2008. It did well and had a second printing before the economy took a nosedive that fall. There was even an option on the book for a TV series, but it never panned out. The bottom line is I finally held my published book in my hands—both hardcover and paperback versions, and I could laugh in the face of that person on the TV show who said women over 40 should probably learn to be content with life just as it is. I remember once at a writer's conference, I was waiting in line to make a pitch of my novel to agents when I saw a fellow writer standing in line, a woman who was about 75 years old. There she was with her cane, weathered face, and gray hair, waiting hopefully to pitch her writing ideas—her dreams—to some wonderboy or wondergirl agent who were all of 30. I remember thinking, "God, don't ever let me be that old and still trying to pursue my dream. Take the dream away before I get that old." I couldn't imagine living the rest of my life still trying in vain to achieve something that meant so much to me.

I meant that then, but as I get older, I realized that woman was doing what we all should do: never giving up on a dream. We all need to pursue our dreams to give us a deeper purpose and meaning to our lives. However old you are, whatever the dream is. Whether it's running a 5K, learning how to swim, singing at karaoke night, losing weight, or growing a beautiful garden.

A number of years ago, when I got together for a rare dinner out with my two of my long-time friends, Ann and Donna. Ann started the conversation with her eyes sparkling and her face glowing. "Y'all," she said breathlessly, hardly able to contain her excitement, "I've decided to do something that I've always wanted to do." She paused, and Donna and I exchanged glances. Was she going on some mountain climbing expedition? Or having plastic surgery? Or going out with a guy ten years younger? Was she going back to school or moving to Europe? After her dramatic pause, Ann took a deep breath, and said, "I'm going to sell Tupperware."

For a split second, there was complete silence. Then Donna and I both burst out laughing. We immediately felt bad about it because of course we supported our friend in what she wanted to do, but we just hadn't been expecting Tupperware. Luckily, Ann understood our reaction. Ann is very outgoing and organized, exactly the kind of person a Tupperware salesperson should be. She is also a banking executive, and selling Tupperware would be something she would do on the side for fun. It was one of her dreams, one that began from those times her mother used to have Tupperware parties where all the women had so much fun socializing together. Donna and I were glad that she had decided to do something she'd put on hold for so long.

My mother's sister, Mary, has always been an inspiration to me and to everyone who knows her. Her two sons are close to my age, and we were very close while growing up; they, and my other cousins, were like siblings to me. Aunt Mary is a very devout Christian woman who practices what she preaches. At the age of 80, she decided she wanted to go on a church mission trip to Ethiopia for two weeks. Lots of people, including me, didn't want her to go because we were worried about her; but, this trip was something she'd always wanted to do, so no one and nothing deterred her. She had a wonderful time over there, made many friends, and helped to reach out to the people there who all called her Mama Mary. It went so well that she decided to go back about a year and a half later. In the interim, she'd had some heart trouble and had to have a pacemaker. Some people asked her in shock, "Mary, are you going to go to Ethiopia with that pacemaker?"

Aunt Mary responded, "Well, I sure can't go without it."

It's that kind of spunk and that kind of determination that we need when pursuing our dreams and goals.

I love to listen to the soundtrack of the play, *Avenue Q*, and there are two lines from two songs in it that make me contemplate the pursuit of our dreams. The first line is from "There's a Fine, Fine Line" and it says, "*Ya gotta go for what you want while you're still in your prime/*" And I find myself wondering what exactly 'prime' is. When does one's prime end? I agree that a person needs to go after what they want while all their cylinders are clicking; but, I also think they should never stop going after what they want, even when most of their cylinders could use a little oil. Even when we're older, we shouldn't stop going for our dreams. And when you're a mom of a certain age who has put your children and your family ahead of your own desires for so long, then there is definitely no statute of limitations on dreams.

Another line I find bittersweet is from "I Wish I Could Go Back to College": *You sit in the quad and think "Oh my God, I am totally gonna go far"/ How do I go back to college?/ I don't know who I am anymore/"* I used to put the soundtrack of this play in the CD player in our SUV and listen to it on the way home from the grocery store—before I would return to my family and the chaos. I'd sing along to it as I pulled into the garage. This was my transition time: going from the 'dreamer' me as I had been in college to the 'mom' me. I wanted to stay in touch with that part of me because when you stop chasing your dreams, you lose yourself somewhere along the way.

But it is difficult to chase dreams while in the midst of raising children, being a wife, going to work, fulfilling your responsibilities, doing the chores, and running the errands. Sometimes it doesn't appear you're making any progress at all. That's why one of my all-time favorite quotes is from Jacob August Riis: "When nothing seems to help, I go and look at a stonecutter hammering away at his rock perhaps a hundred times without as much as a crack showing in it. Yet at the hundred and first blow it will split in two, and I know it was not that blow that did it, but all that had gone before."

Go for it, ladies. Break through the stone.

In Dog Years

Our red long-haired dachshund named Fenway, has been the light of our family's life for 13 years. He can make a good day great and a bad day a lot better. Sure, he's awfully cute with his floppy ears, but it's his personality that truly won us over. "Like a member of the family" is a trite phrase that is probably overused to attempt to describe how people feel about their pets. But within a few days of having Fen, we all knew exactly what that phrase meant. There was nothing trite or insincere about it.

We get so incredibly attached to our pets, and they hold a special place in our hearts, deservedly so. And when our pets face a health issue, we realize—if we didn't already—just how much we love them. That happened to us back when Fenway was seven. He started shivering and was reluctant to walk as if it hurt him. Dachshunds, with their long backs and short legs, are prone to back problems, and that was what we feared Fen's problem was. We took him to the NC State Veterinary School and had an MRI done, which showed Fen had a herniated disc. Our options were to have him rest a lot in his crate while taking pain meds or for Fen to have surgery. The idea of Fenway relying on pain medications for the rest of his life was hard to accept since he was only 7-years-old and would hopefully live a much longer time. I'd had a dachshund when I was growing up and he lived until the age of 16.

Besides, his back problem could get worse, possibly resulting in paralysis of his back legs and hind end. So we opted for the surgery. The doctors told us that if the disc had been herniated for a while that it might be impossible to get it totally out of the spinal canal but that they could increase the space around the herniated disc to give the disc more room to move without hitting nerves. They could also do a preventative procedure on the other discs in his back to ward off problems in the future.

The night before the surgery, we were extremely glad we'd decided on the surgery because Fenway's breathing was very labored, groaning with each breath, obviously in tremendous pain. We took him into the vet school, and the surgery began around noon. We waited for a phone call they said would come around four o'clock. Finally, the news came: Fenway had come through surgery well, but they could not get the herniated disc out of the spinal canal because it was embedded too well and would be too risky to Fenway's spine. But they did do the other two procedures, which would hopefully be enough to keep him pain-free for a long time. (And it has for the most part.)

My oldest son, Billy, then 20, and I went to visit him the next day since Kevin was away on business. We knew that it would be a shock to see him again since he'd be so wobbly after major surgery. And we knew his back would be shaved somewhat. When we got to his kennel area, he took a step toward us, excited, and then plopped down on his butt. Cute if he were a puppy learning to walk, but scary when he was an adult dog with back problems. They also had shaved a lot more of his back than we thought they would. His back was totally furless, and there was about an eight inch incision down his back complete with stitches and staples. It was a rather shocking sight. But Fen was so happy to see us, and we were overjoyed to see him. To hold him. To let him know that we were still there for him even though he had to stay at the hospital another night.

I thought Jason, our 11-year-old, was going to faint the first time he saw Fenway when we brought him home. Jason's face froze and went pale, and his eyes did something I can't really describe; they somehow lost their sparkle and looked glossed over in disbelief. Billy and I both asked him if he was all right. He said he was, but then he put his head in my lap beside Fen and burst into uncontrollable tears. I shed some tears too, and when I looked at Billy, sure enough, there were tears brimming in his eyes also. Jason later said that he had expected to see stitches in Fen's back, but not staples, and that took him by surprise.

Throughout the whole month of December, we couldn't let Fen move around a lot—and certainly not play or climb stairs. We either held him or put him in his crate; we carried him around from room to room and outside to his pen to do his business. We'd take turns holding him during the day and at night he slept in his wire crate right in the middle of our king size bed. He was under constant supervision. It was like having a baby again. We also had to give him medications three times a day for three weeks. Fen's days of going up and down steps were gone, and so for the past six years, we've carried him up and down the stairs in our house and down our deck steps.

Soon after Fenway's surgery, I sat down beside him on the deck and watched him as he basked in the sun, sometimes distracted by a squirrel. He'd give a half-hearted bark and then hold his nose up toward the sun and partially close his eyes like that sunshine felt so good. I'd had back surgery myself several years earlier, and he was now going through getting older just as I have been. It was then I realized that in dog years, Fen was 49—just like I was at the time. I put my arm around him and sighed. "Being 49 sucks, doesn't it, Fen?" He turned to me and licked my face. I think he was saying our best years are still ahead.

Perspective

Back in 2013, I went in for my regularly scheduled mammogram breast screening—something women don't look forward to having done but that we have to do. I opted to have the new 3D screening since it provided better views for the doctor to read, which resulted in fewer callbacks for re-checks of mammograms. In the past, I'd been called back twice to be re-checked, and I didn't want to go through the stress of waiting for a second mammogram. The 3D version was $50 more, but I'd gladly pay that for a more definitive exam that would lessen my chances of getting called back in because something 'looked' suspicious on the exam but wasn't clear.

While I was having the 3D exam, the X-ray technician made awkward conversation with me in talking about the weather and sports teams—he kind of talk that I'm sure was an unwanted trademark of her job. Then she mentioned that when it was time for her mammogram, that she would also want to have a 3D exam like I was doing. I told her that I was glad it reduced the chances of coming back in, and her response was, "And if they do call a person back in after a 3D exam, then it will probably be much more serious of a concern." I didn't reply to her comment because at that time my left boob was being smashed in between two plastic plates. But I did remember it.

So when I got a call two days later that I needed to come back in for further screening, I thought immediately of the technician's comment. I got a sick feeling. Especially when they couldn't get me another appointment until Tuesday afternoon and it was only Thursday. I'd have to wait over the weekend, which is the pits because the thought of it is always hanging over your head. I couldn't believe I'd have to wait that long when I'd been a patient at the radiology center for over a decade and needed to be rechecked. I tried unsuccessfully to get an earlier appointment, even telling them of the comment the technician had made to me and how it was unsettling to me. Later that afternoon, my doctor called to reassure me. She told me that they had already had to send several other women who had had 3D mammograms back for rechecks and they had all been okay. That did indeed make me feel better. I stayed busy all through the weekend and kept in mind what my doctor had said.

When I got to the clinic on Tuesday, I dressed in the familiar oh-so-attractive gown with the tie-strings and waited in the room with other women in the same gowns, all with our plastic drawstring bags filled with our clothes at our feet. We waited for our name to be called. When mine was called, I followed the technician back into the office. After the obligatory, "How are you today?" from her, there were more photos, more squeezing and squishing of the boobs. You know the routine. Afterwards, she had me return to the waiting area and told me that the doctor would look at the images and if there were concerns, I'd have an ultrasound. About ten minutes later, she returned and simply said—there in front of the other women—"Mrs. O'Donnell, you need to go down the hall and see our ultrasound specialist." Oh, crap, I thought. That's not good.

While I was having the ultrasound, I remembered the happy times when I'd had ultrasounds when I was pregnant with my 3 sons, how it'd felt to see the strange outlines of their little bodies when they were inside me, how miraculous it was to see them move and later, to hear their heartbeats. It was odd to think of the joy I'd felt in such a similar situation compared to what I was feeling now.

I tried to read the reaction of the technician's face when she was looking at the ultrasound, but I couldn't. Then she stood up quickly and said something about 'dear' followed by, "I'm going to go talk to the doctor about this and I'll be right back." I nodded, and she was out the door.

The room was painfully quiet. She'd said something that ended with 'dear'. Had she said 'oh, dear' or was it 'okay dear'? They always called women getting mammograms 'sweetie' and 'dear' so I was hoping she'd said, "Okay, dear, I'm going to talk to the doctor." Surely, she would not have said 'oh dear' as if she were alarmed. These are the kinds of things that run through your head while waiting for such news.

I'd thought she'd return within a minute or two, but it was longer. After almost ten minutes went by, I took a deep breath and blew it out slowly. "Okay," I thought to myself, "this is taking a long time. If it is bad news, I have to get ready for it." And then in my mind, I began to plan. I definitely still wanted to take my youngest son to New York City the following week, just as we'd planned. Surely, whatever treatment I'd need could wait a week. Then I thought about how it would be to tell my sons the bad news, and I knew I would have to be as positive about it as I could be so they wouldn't worry and let it affect them. Why not me? I thought to myself. And my stream of thoughts went like this: Women get this diagnosis every day, unfortunately. Why, logically, would I NOT be affected by breast cancer at some point in my life? Let's start chemo right away, let's have the lumpectomy or whatever right away—just let me be there for my boys for a long time. I couldn't allow myself to be devastated by any bad news; I wanted to take it in stride and to remember all those who have had to go through this themselves.

Then "Why Not Me?," a country music hit of The Judds, started running through my mind. Just the chorus, not the verses—just repeating the question, "Why Not Me?" I used to work at a country radio station when the song first came out, and the lyrics and melody came to me immediately after the thought occurred to me. I took another deep breath and contemplated how I'd break the news to my husband after I left here and went by his office. Would I then post a note on Facebook and ask for prayers or would I keep it private for a while? I didn't know what would be the best thing to do.

And then the door opened and in came the ultrasound technician ... followed by the doctor. That couldn't be good, I knew. *Ask good questions,* I remember thinking. *I need to stay calm.* The doctor extended her hand to me and introduced herself. "I wanted to take a look myself," the doctor said, as she sat on the stool and looked at the monitor. "But everything looks good."

Did she really just say that? I asked myself. Everything looks good? It sounded like I was hearing under water, the words distorted. The words were not what I was expecting, not the words I'd built myself up to be prepared for. So I repeated them back to her: "Everything looks good?"

"Yes," she replied. "You see that black area here on the screen." I turned my head to look at the monitor and nodded, but I actually didn't see anything. I was too relieved to concentrate on what showed on the monitor. It could have been a photo of Humpty-Dumpty up there and I wouldn't have noticed. She continued to explain: "That's a cyst. That's new from your screening last year, more than just dense breast tissue." I nodded again, and I think I made an "Um-huh" noise, but I'm not sure. Inside my mind, I kept saying a silent, "Thank you, God" over and over.

The doctor went on to explain more in detail, saying "It has all 3 things that a cyst is supposed to have, not 1 of 3 or 2 of 3, but all 3, so I'm not concerned at all."

"So it doesn't have to be removed?" I managed to ask.

"Not unless it causes you pain and you want it out." I'd never felt any pain there, and it was not a concern of mine right then. So I nodded yet again. The doctor smiled and told me to just come back in for my regular exam the following year.

And that was it. Time to take off the gown, put back on the clothes from my plastic bag. As I went back out into the lobby, my heart was light, my steps were light. When I went outside, the sun was shining. Or maybe it was cloudy. I honestly don't remember. Because to me, the sun was shining brightly.

They Call Me Mom

Although I have three children, sometimes it's still difficult for me to think of myself as a mother. Even after 26 years of being one. Of course I love my boys and try to teach them right from wrong. I've helped them with their homework, stood in long lines to sign them up for swim lessons and other events, taught their Sunday school classes, made their favorite meals, done their laundry, advocated for them when I think they've been treated unfairly, disciplined them when they need it, cheered at so many of their sports events that I can't remember the name of their team, joked with them, tucked them in at night, and have always said a quick prayer for them as I stopped by their rooms later to watch them sleep. I've changed their diapers, comforted them after nightmares, and read aloud "Good Night Moon" and Curious George books. I've sacrificed sleep, sacrificed money, & sacrificed my desires for theirs many times. All this and yet, I feel like the word 'motherhood' is reserved for a special brand of people much more deserving of the name than I am.

I suppose my own mother has set such a high standard of being a mom that I feel I haven't reached that level yet. My mother, or 'Mama' as we usually call her, could put to shame June Cleaver, Harriet Nelson, and Carol Brady without breaking a sweat. She's a great cook, whipping up her specialties like pineapple cake, chicken salad, or homemade yeast rolls that are famous among her family and friends. She was very involved with the PTA and in our classes, letting her four children see the high value she placed on education. We also watched and learned as she has done a lot of volunteer work in her church, how she likes to visit people who are sick or maybe just need to talk. Mama continues this work today even though she's 93 years old. She stays active, even though she can no longer drive because of bad eyesight due to macular degeneration. Up until a few years ago, she could out-walk anybody in the mall, but recent hip and leg problems have slowed her down. Mama used to pitch baseballs to her grandchildren when they were growing up, and even though her mobility was not the best, she did this with Jason, her youngest grandchild, too.

There are only a few times in my childhood that I can remember her becoming impatient with any of us. Same thing with my dad. Both of them have been wonderful parents. It seems I used to go through at least two episodes of impatience with my children each day. I remember Mama calling out my spelling words to me the night before a test—how calm and encouraging her voice was. I can recall Daddy trying in vain to explain math to me, how he'd calmly take me through the steps and then look at my blank face and realize I still didn't understand. He'd simply start over with another approach by saying, "In other words ..."

But of course since I am a mom, I compare myself to my mother and find myself thinking about memories that epitomize for me the wonderful mother she's been, There have been times one of my children was upset, and as I hugged them, held them, & tried to console them, I suddenly realized they needed me just the way I needed

Mama when I ran to her when I was little. That faith, that trust that she'd make everything better was what *my* children were feeling about me. It scared me when that realization would come over me—that I should be for them what Mama was for me. Those are big footsteps for me to follow in.

Sometimes it's the small things I remember that epitomize her love and caring. There was the time I was a freshman in college, feeling so lonely and so different on a campus with 20,000 others. Parties were all over the place, people were getting drunk, and I felt out of place. I'd call home when I'd get really depressed. The phone would ring a few times and then that oh so comforting voice would say "Hello?" I'd pause a second before I spoke, just savoring her voice.

"Mama, it's me," I'd say, before pouring my heart out to her.

There were the times our family would get into the station wagon and head to the beach or Grandma's house. On those trips, I remember my mother sitting in the passenger seat beside my father with her left arm stretched out along the top of the seat. Occasionally, she'd turn her head to check on us kids; then satisfied that everything was okay, she'd turn back around with a smile on her face. That arm along the front seat signaled to me that everything was in control, everything was going as expected. It was a good feeling.

As we sat on the third row of the small Presbyterian church where I grew up, Mama would tap her shoe on the shiny linoleum floor in rhythm to the organist playing "Amazing Grace" or some other favorite hymn. She didn't tap her shoe along with all the songs—only the ones she really liked. I can hear that sound in my mind even now. It taught me a lot about her spirit, her soul, her music.

Once when Billy was a baby, he and I both had fevers at the same time. It was hard to take care of him when I was feeling so bad myself. So I called Mama and asked if she could come over and take care of him while I got some rest. Naturally, she said yes. While I waited for her to get to my house, I lay down on the bed with Billy on my chest, listening for the sound of her at the door. A little while later, I heard the front door open and her voice say, "Knock, knock." What a welcome sound that was! I met her at the top of the stairs and handed Billy to her, and then I climbed into the bed to sleep. Mama was there. All was right.

The role of mom is a huge role to fill, and I hope I've done an adequate enough job of filling it, but I will always pale in comparison to my own mother. I hope I've been able to convey the essence and comfort of motherhood to my boys at least half as well as Mama conveyed it to me.

Every now and then, I get some hints that I'm not a total failure. Once I was out of town for a night at a book reading to promote my first book. When I returned home, six-year-old Jason hugged me and looked at me with sad eyes. "Mom, when you're not home, I feel like I'm all alone," he said softly. My heart melted, but I also felt terrible for leaving him. With just Kevin and the older two boys there with him, I knew he probably didn't get much nurturing and perhaps had to even fend for food by himself. But I had no idea Jason had felt this badly. I told Kevin that Jason said he felt alone when I wasn't there that night. "There was a baseball game on TV," he replied, as if that explained everything.

And as we travel down the road of life, I can't help but contemplate the lessons of life I'd like my boys to take along with them. Growing up, my boys each had a poster in their rooms that has a photo of a baseball player lying on the ground with his glove outstretched, and you can tell he just barely caught the ball. A miraculous catch. The Bible verse underneath the photo is Philippians 4:13: *I can do all things through Christ who strengthens me.* This is a Bible verse that I want my boys to remember and to repeat to themselves in challenging times. Because there have been and will be challenging times.

My mother can't drive any longer so she doesn't come to my house very often now. But I cherish the memories of those days when she'd drop by, of hearing her cheerful voice saying "knock, knock" as she tapped on the door. It's hard to be a mother and at the same time to watch your own mother reach her 90s because suddenly the cycle of life is all too clear. I want to hang on to my kids and hang on to my parents when I can hang on to neither. But there are some awfully good moments along the way. My mother used to say that time goes by so much faster as you get older. I used to doubt that when I was younger because logically time should pass at the same speed regardless of one's age. But Mama, you were right. You were right.

Being an older mom is not so bad. Motherhood truly is a wonderful gift. At any age. Sure, when you have a baby when you're over 38, you do subconsciously hope that someone gives you a facelift gift certificate at your baby shower to be used when you feel a dire need to fit in with the younger moms. But being an older mom certainly has its blessings, too. With Billy and David now college graduates and pursuing their own goals and dreams, I'm so thankful I have good relationships with them and that I still have my Jason at home a little longer. I don't really mind that Kevin and I might be the oldest couple on the sidelines at Jason's last games in high school; in fact, I like cheering him on. And he has provided me with moments of encouragement along the way. Jason said to me once when he was seven, "I love you, Mom, even though you're old aged." Thanks sweetheart, I needed that ... I think.

Forever Young

I know that parenthood is all about raising your children so that they are independent and can fly off on their own, ready to face the world and be successful. And of course, I want that for my kids. Any parent would. I've been lucky that my two oldest sons have succeeded while also staying close to home; they went to college 15 minutes away, and my oldest son's first job was here in the same town that they grew up in, and the middle one has accepted a job here also to begin next year after he finishes his Master's program. Although my nest was emptying, with only my high schooler still left a home, they weren't flying very far away. We could still meet for lunch or dinner, and holidays were always easy to plan due to the lack of travel.

In 2017, though, my oldest son, Billy, decided to move five hours away to Washington, D.C. Not that far away from Raleigh, but still—it is AWAY. He is the first one to leave this town we have all thought of as 'home'. He went to a Master's program at the University of Virginia a few years ago, but we knew he'd be coming back home afterwards, so Charlottesville didn't have the permanence written all over it like D.C. does. I can certainly understand the allure of Washington: it's a mecca for young, single professionals, and one of his good friends from UVA already lives there (and of course, there is a professional baseball team). I'm honestly excited for him, and I loved hearing about his new life there. With texting, he can live in D.C. and I still feel like he's only 15 minutes away. The bottom line is that I want him to be happy. I've been with him when he has been pretty low, and I know that his being happy is the most important thing.

I want my sons to pursue dreams and have adventures, but my heart is always with them. When David, my middle son, was flying to Prague for a study abroad grad school course in 2017, I couldn't sleep. I knew he'd be arriving at two in the morning our time, and so I stayed awake until then. I went on the Internet to the Flight Tracking site where you can find flights and 'see' the plane as it travels, see it on its journey and as it reaches its destination. I've always been a big believer in visualization; when I'm praying for people during certain times or events, I close my eyes and see in my mind's eye where they are at that time, imagine them in their surroundings, and then I imagine God looking at them, too, taking them in the palm of His hand, holding them safely. The tracking website helped me with that visualization process, to see in my mind the plane touching down as it landed. And it helped give me peace.

Jason will be graduating from high school soon, off to find his path and his passion. My caboose baby is not a baby any longer. I've been taking those college tours with him recently like I did with my older boys, but this time I'm suffering from hot flashes in the crowded rooms and foot problems as we trek across campus. The plight of the older mom. It's come full circle, as I recall those elementary days of PTA meetings. This time, though, unlike when Jason was in elementary school, I don't care or even notice if I'm the oldest mom there, and chances are these days, I'm not the oldest mom there. Older moms are indeed a growing group across the nation, the world, in PTAs, and on the college tours. Yes, ladies, we fit right in now.

Even though my sons might be flying—literally and figuratively—they still must touch down every now and then. To be grounded again, to rediscover their roots. And when they do, they need to find the faith and encouragement to venture to fly again. That's what home is for. That's what I'm for.

When Billy was in the first grade, he wrote on a picture he drew of the earth that Kevin and I—his parents—made his world spin around. It made my heart melt when I read it, but at the same time, I was overwhelmed with the responsibility I felt for him. Jason wrote at the same age in a booklet for school, "My mom makes me laugh. I love the sound of happiness." These are the kind of things I treasure so much, and yes, I have a whole wooden chest crammed pack with school projects and pictures, and I'm glad I do even though I might wind up on that Hoarders show in the future.

There is an essay David wrote in the first grade that I think sums up being a mom pretty well—from his perspective. He wrote, "My mom does a lot of things for me. She helps me when I am hurt. She takes care of me. She cooks food for me. She takes me places like the mall and the dentist. She helps me pass tests and get great grades. She lays down with me and my brother Billy at night time. When I am alone, she holds me. She goes on field trips with me. She does this for me because she loves me."

As a mom, no matter what my age is, I will always see my boys in my mind as these little boys who wrote these words, who filled my life with laughter and love. Yes, my family dynamics are changing as my sons grow older and so do my husband and I; the empty nest is drawing near. As an older mom, I might sometimes lament the fact that age takes a toll on my body and sometimes my mind and spirit; yes, it would be nice to be forever young. Of course, I know that's not possible, and that's okay. It is my sons who will always be forever young to me, and that is what I cherish. Moms know what I'm talking about.

When Billy and David graduated from high school, I made videos with photos and home video excerpts along with accompanying songs, and I will do the same for Jason. One of the songs I chose for this is *Forever Young* by Bob Dylan and Rod Stewart as the lyrics are quite appropriate to express my feelings about our kids growing up. The song reflects on the hopes that all parents should have for their child—hopes that the child will grow up to be happy, strong, and loved, that the child will always be kind to others and true to oneself, and that God will be with their child throughout life. The chorus ends with the words: "And in my heart you'll always stay ... forever young." Part of them will always be our little boys or little girls, their innocent faces frozen in time, their sweet voices echoing in our minds.

Why do moms of all ages feel this way? I think David sums it up best in the last sentence of his first grade essay when he wrote, "Nobody can love me like my mother."

And, no, it doesn't matter at all how old the mother is.

About the Author

S haron O'Donnell, a native North Carolinian, is a graduate of the University of North Carolina at Chapel Hill with a degree in print/broadcast journalism.

Sharon's debut title, *House of Testosterone—One Mom's Survival in a Household of Males*, was named a notable book by IndieBound. From 1998-2010, she wrote a regular column for The Cary News that won several statewide awards in North Carolina. Her writing has also been featured in Good Housekeeping, Better Homes & Gardens, The News & Observer (Raleigh, NC), and Blue Mountain Arts greeting cards.

Sharon lives in Cary, NC with her husband, Kevin, their youngest son, Jason, 17, and their 13-year-old long-haired dachshund, with frequent visits from sons Bill, 26, and David, 24. In addition to her own websites, Sharon is a blogger for www.motherhoodlater.com, the leading website for older moms.

Connect with Sharon:

www.sharonodonnellauthor.com
www.momsofboys.org
www.uplit.org
Twitter: @4boysanddog

Resources

National PTA:

www.pta.org: website for national PTA that contains links to all state offices, information about issues and programs, and much more.

www.facebook.com/ParentTeacherAssociation

Websites:

www.sharonodonnellauthor.com: Sharon's site that includes a look at her book, Please Don't Let Me Be the Oldest Mom in the PTA! and other resources for older moms.

www.achildafter40.com: The truth about motherhood after 40, primarily getting pregnant after 40-- resources, social groups, and a blog by founder Angel La Liberte.

www.advancedmaternalage.org: provides information and support for women who chose to start their families after the age of 35.

www.forwomenoverforty.com: Fetures great audio/radio interviews (88.1 fm, broadcast at WESU) regarding subjects for women over 40. Founder, Cyma Shapiro who also founded motheringinthemiddle.com *www.inseasonmom.org:* for older moms who know there are seasons of life for everything. Features stories of moms over 35. Site founder, Cynthia Wilson James

www.menopausalmom.com: Musings on the good, the bad and the ugly side of midlife mayhem.

www.momsofboys.org/older-moms-page: a page of Sharon's momsofboys.org site dedicated to older moms, including humor, book excerpts, videos, and articles.

www.motherhoodlater.com (motherhood later ... not sooner): for moms who become mothers later in life -- for first-time moms as well as those women who become moms again later in life. Features interviews, blogs, and social groups. Founder, Robin Gorman Newman. And Sharon is a blogger on the site www.motherhoodlater.com/?s=Sharon

www.motheringinthemiddle.com: for midlife mothers and midlife fathers, Site founder, Cyma Shapiro.

www.mothersoverforty.com: by the author of Hot Flashes, Warm Bottles, Nancy London.

Books:

Blackstone-Ford, Jann (2002). *Midlife Motherhood: A Woman-to-Woman Guide to Pregnancy and Parenting.* New York: St. Martin's Press.

Gregory, Elizabeth (2007). *Ready: Why Women Are Embracing the New Later Motherhood.* Philadelphia: Perseus Books Group.

Lavin, Ellen, PhD (1998). *The Essential Over 35 Pregnancy Guide.* New York: Avon Books.

London, Nancy (2001). *Hot Flashes, Warm Bottles: First Time Mothers Over 40*. Berkeley, CA: Ten Speed Press.

McGraw, Robin (2010). *What's Age Got to Do with It?: Living Your Happiest and Healthiest Life*. Nashville, TN: Thomas Nelson, Inc.

Nagle, Doreen (2002). *But I Don't Feel Too Old to Be a Mommy!: The Complete Sourcebook for Starting (and Re-Starting) Motherhood Beyond 35 and After 40*. Deerfield Beach, FL: Health Communications.

Shanahan, Kelly M., M.D. (2001). *Your Over-35 Week-by-Week Pregnancy Guide: All the Answers to All Your Questions About Pregnancy, Birth, and Your Developing Baby*. New York: Three Rivers Press.

Shapiro, Cyma (2013). *The Zen of Midlife Mothering: Essays from MotheringintheMiddle.com*. Charleston, SC: CreateSpace.

Facebook Groups and Pages:

First Time Moms Over 40: www.facebook.com/groups/916068721815796

Menopausal Mother: www.facebook.com/Menopausal-Mother

Moms Over 40 with Infants, Toddlers, and Young Children: www.facebook.com/groups/166428086710464

Moms Over 40: www.facebook.com/moms-over-40-64817389954

Older Adoptive Moms: www.facebook.com/groups/170099893560885

Older Moms and Munchkins Club: www.facebook.com/
groups/379324652086552

Older Moms of Young Children: www.facebook.com/
groups/243241469078727

Older Moms Rock!: www.facebook.com/
groups/234020170100596

Older Moms Support Group 35 Plus: www.facebook.
com/groups/204468553279545

The Advanced Maternal Age Project: www.facebook.
com/AdvancedMaternalAge

CPSIA information can be obtained
at www.ICGtesting.com
Printed in the USA
FFOW02n0651080618
47041686-49338FF